THE ALEXANDER SHA

General Editor
R.B. Kennedy

Additional notes and editing
Mike Gould

THE TAMING OF
THE SHREW

William Shakespeare

COLLINS
CL

Harper Press
An imprint of HarperCollins*Publishers*
77–85 Fulham Palace Road
Hammersmith
London W6 8JB

This Harper Press paperback edition published 2011

A catalogue record for this book is available from the British Library

ISBN: 978-0-00-793443-0

Printed and bound in Great Britain by Clays Ltd, St Ives plc

MIX
Paper from
responsible sources
FSC® C007454

Life & Times section © Gerard Cheshire
Introduction by Dorothy McMillan
Shakespeare: Words and Phrases adapted from
Collins English Dictionary
Typesetting in Kalix by Palimpsest Book Production Limited,
Falkirk, Stirlingshire

10 9 8 7 6 5 4 3 2 1

Prefatory Note

This Shakespeare play uses the full Alexander text. By keeping in mind the fact that the language has changed considerably in four hundred years, as have customs, jokes, and stage conventions, the editors have aimed at helping the modern reader – whether English is their mother tongue or not – to grasp the full significance of the play. The Notes, intended primarily for examination candidates, are presented in a simple, direct style. The needs of those unfamiliar with British culture have been specially considered.

Since quiet study of the printed word is unlikely to bring fully to life plays that were written directly for the public theatre, attention has been drawn to dramatic effects which are important in performance. The editors see Shakespeare's plays as living works of art which can be enjoyed today on stage, film and television in many parts of the world.

CONTENTS

An Elizabethan playhouse. Note the apron stage protruding into the auditorium, the space below it, the inner room at the rear of the stage, the gallery above the inner stage, the canopy over the main stage, and the absence of a roof over the audience.

The Theatre in Shakespeare's Day

On the face of it, the conditions in the Elizabethan theatre were not such as to encourage great writers. The public playhouse itself was not very different from an ordinary inn-yard; it was open to the weather; among the spectators were often louts, pickpockets and prostitutes; some of the actors played up to the rowdy elements in the audience by inserting their own jokes into the authors' lines, while others spoke their words loudly but unfeelingly; the presentation was often rough and noisy, with fireworks to represent storms and battles, and a table and a few chairs to represent a tavern; there were no actresses, so boys took the parts of women, even such subtle and mature ones as Cleopatra and Lady Macbeth; there was rarely any scenery at all in the modern sense. In fact, a quick inspection of the English theatre in the reign of Elizabeth I by a time-traveller from the twentieth century might well produce only one positive reaction: the costumes were often elaborate and beautiful.

Shakespeare himself makes frequent comments in his plays about the limitations of the playhouse and the actors of his time, often apologizing for them. At the beginning of *Henry V* the Prologue refers to the stage as 'this unworthy scaffold' and to the theatre building (the Globe, probably) as 'this wooden O', and emphasizes the urgent need for imagination in making up for all the deficiencies of presentation. In introducing Act IV the Chorus goes so far as to say:

> . . . we shall much disgrace
> With four or five most vile and ragged foils,
> Right ill-dispos'd in brawl ridiculous,
> The name of Agincourt, (lines 49–52)

In *A Midsummer Night's Dream* (Act V, Scene i) he seems to dismiss actors with the words:

The best in this kind are but shadows.

Yet Elizabeth's theatre, with all its faults, stimulated dramatists to a variety of achievement that has never been equalled and, in Shakespeare, produced one of the greatest writers in history. In spite of all his grumbles he seems to have been fascinated by the challenge that it presented him with. It is necessary to re-examine his theatre carefully in order to understand how he was able to achieve so much with the materials he chose to use. What sort of place was the Elizabethan playhouse in reality? What sort of people were these criticized actors? And what sort of audiences gave them their living?

The Development of the Theatre up to Shakespeare's Time

For centuries in England noblemen had employed groups of skilled people to entertain them when required. Under Tudor rule, as England became more secure and united, actors such as these were given more freedom, and they often performed in public, while still acknowledging their 'overlords' (in the 1570s, for example, when Shakespeare was still a schoolboy at Stratford, one famous company was called 'Lord Leicester's Men'). London was rapidly becoming larger and more important in the second half of the sixteenth century, and many of the companies of actors took the opportunities offered to establish themselves at inns on the main roads leading to the City (for example, the Boar's Head in Whitechapel and the Tabard in South-wark) or in the City itself. These groups of actors would come to an agreement with the inn-keeper which would give them the use of the yard for their performances after people had eaten and drunk well in the middle of the day. Before long, some inns were taken over completely by companies of players and thus became the first public theatres. In 1574 the officials of the City of London issued an order which shows clearly that these theatres were both popular and also offensive to some respectable people, because the order complains about 'the inordinate haunting of great multitudes of people, specially youth, to plays interludes and shows; namely occasion of frays and quarrels, evil practices of incontinency in great inns . . .' There is evidence that, on public holidays, the theatres on the banks of the Thames were crowded with noisy apprentices and tradesmen, but it would be wrong to think that audiences were always undiscriminating and loudmouthed. In spite of the disapproval of Puritans and the more staid members of society, by the 1590s, when Shakespeare's plays were beginning to be performed, audiences consisted of a good cross-section of English society, nobility as well as workers, intellectuals as well as simple people out for a laugh; also (and in this respect English theatres were unique in Europe), it was quite normal for respectable women to attend plays. So Shakespeare had to write plays which would appeal to people of widely different kinds. He had to provide 'something for everyone' but at the same time to take care to unify the material so that it would not seem to fall into separate pieces as they watched it. A speech like that of the drunken porter in *Macbeth* could provide the 'groundlings' with a belly-laugh, but also held a deeper significance for those who could appreciate it. The audience he wrote for was one of a number of apparent drawbacks which Shakespeare was able to turn to his and our advantage.

Shakespeare's Actors

Nor were all the actors of the time mere 'rogues, vagabonds and sturdy beggars' as some were described in a Statute of 1572. It is true that many of them had a hard life and earned very little money, but leading actors could become partners in the ownership of the theatres in which they acted: Shakespeare was a shareholder in the Globe and the Blackfriars theatres when he was an actor as well as a playwright. In any case, the attacks made on Elizabethan actors were usually directed at their morals and not at their acting ability; it is clear that many of them must have been good at their trade if they were able to interpret complex works like the great tragedies in such a way as to attract enthusiastic audiences. Undoubtedly some of the boys took the women's parts with skill and confidence, since a man called Coryate, visiting Venice in 1611, expressed surprise that women could act as well as they: 'I saw women act, a thing that I never saw before . . . and they performed it with as good a grace, action, gesture . . . as ever I saw any masculine actor.' The quality of most of the actors who first presented Shakespeare's plays is probably accurately summed up by Fynes Moryson, who wrote, '. . . as there be, in my opinion, more plays in London than in all the parts of the world I have seen, so do these players or comedians excel all other in the world.'

The Structure of the Public Theatre

Although the 'purpose-built' theatres were based on the inn-yards which had been used for play-acting, most of them were circular. The walls contained galleries on three storeys from which the wealthier patrons watched, they must have been something like the 'boxes' in a modern theatre, except that they held much larger numbers – as many as 1500. The 'groundlings' stood on the floor of the building, facing a raised stage which projected from the 'stage-wall', the main features of which were:

1 a small room opening on to the back of the main stage and on the same level as it (rear stage),
2 a gallery above this inner stage (upper stage),
3 canopy projecting from above the gallery over the main stage, to protect the actors from the weather (the 700 or 800 members of the audience who occupied the yard, or 'pit' as we call it today, had the sky above them).

In addition to these features there were dressing-rooms behind the stage and a space underneath it from which entrances could be made through trap-doors. All the acting areas – main stage, rear stage, upper stage and under stage – could be entered by actors directly from their dressing rooms, and all of them were used in productions of Shakespeare's plays. For example, the inner stage, an almost cavelike structure, would have been where Ferdinand and Miranda are 'discovered' playing chess in the last act of *The Tempest*, while the upper stage was certainly the balcony from which Romeo climbs down in Act III of *Romeo and Juliet*.

It can be seen that such a building, simple but adaptable, was not really unsuited to the presentation of plays like Shakespeare's. On the contrary, its simplicity guaranteed the minimum of distraction, while its shape and construction must have produced a sense of involvement on the part of the audience that modern producers would envy.

Other Resources of the Elizabethan Theatre

Although there were few attempts at scenery in the public theatre (painted backcloths were occasionally used in court performances), Shakespeare and his fellow playwrights were able to make use of a fair variety of 'properties', lists of such articles have survived: they include beds, tables, thrones, and also trees, walls, a gallows, a Trojan horse and a 'Mouth of Hell'; in a list of properties belonging to the manager, Philip Henslowe, the curious item 'two mossy banks' appears. Possibly one of them was used for the

> bank whereon the wild thyme blows,
> Where oxlips and the nodding violet grows

in *A Midsummer Night's Dream* (Act II, Scene i). Once again, imagination must have been required of the audience.

Costumes were the one aspect of stage production in which

trouble and expense were hardly ever spared to obtain a magnificent effect. Only occasionally did they attempt any historical accuracy (almost all Elizabethan productions were what we should call 'modern-dress' ones), but they were appropriate to the characters who wore them: kings were seen to be kings and beggars were similarly unmistakable. It is an odd fact that there was usually no attempt at illusion in the costuming: if a costume looked fine and rich it probably was. Indeed, some of the costumes were almost unbelievably expensive. Henslowe lent his company £19 to buy a cloak, and the Alleyn brothers, well-known actors, gave £20 for a 'black velvet cloak, with sleeves embroidered all with silver and gold, lined with black satin striped with gold'.

With the one exception of the costumes, the 'machinery' of the playhouse was economical and uncomplicated rather than crude and rough, as we can see from this second and more leisurely look at it. This meant that playwrights were stimulated to produce the imaginative effects that they wanted from the language that they used. In the case of a really great writer like Shakespeare, when he had learned his trade in the theatre as an actor, it seems that he received quite enough assistance of a mechanical and structural kind without having irksome restrictions and conventions imposed on him; it is interesting to try to guess what he would have done with the highly complex apparatus of a modern television studio. We can see when we look back to his time that he used his instrument, the Elizabethan theatre, to the full, but placed his ultimate reliance on the communication between his imagination and that of his audience through the medium of words. It is, above all, his rich and wonderful use of language that must have made play-going at that time a memorable experience for people of widely different kinds. Fortunately, the deep satisfaction of appreciating and enjoying Shakespeare's work can be ours also, if we are willing to overcome the language difficulty produced by the passing of time.

Shakespeare: A Timeline

Very little indeed is known about Shakespeare's private life; the facts included here are almost the only indisputable ones. The dates of Shakespeare's plays are those on which they were first produced.

1558   Queen Elizabeth crowned.

1561   Francis Bacon born.

1564   Christopher Marlowe born.   William Shakespeare born, April 23rd, baptized April 26th.

1566   Shakespeare's brother, Gilbert, born.

1567   Mary, Queen of Scots, deposed.
       James VI (later James I of England) crowned King of Scotland.

1572   Ben Jonson born.
       Lord Leicester's Company (of players) licensed; later called Lord Strange's, then the Lord Chamberlain's and finally (under James) the King's Men.

1573   John Donne born.

1574   The Common Council of London directs that all plays and playhouses in London must be licensed.

1576   James Burbage builds the first public playhouse, The Theatre, at Shoreditch, outside the walls of the City.

1577   Francis Drake begins his voyage round the world (completed 1580).
       Holinshed's Chronicles of England, Scotland and Ireland published (which

	Shakespeare later used extensively).	
1582		Shakespeare married to Anne Hathaway.
1583	The Queen's Company founded by royal warrant.	Shakespeare's daughter, Susanna, born.
1585		Shakespeare's twins, Hamnet and Judith, born.
1586	Sir Philip Sidney, the Elizabethan ideal 'Christian knight', poet, patron, soldier, killed at Zutphen in the Low Countries.	
1587	Mary, Queen of Scots, beheaded. Marlowe's *Tamburlaine (Part I)* first staged.	
1588	Defeat of the Spanish Armada. Marlowe's *Tamburlaine (Part II)* first staged.	
1589	Marlowe's *Jew of Malta* and Kyd's *Spanish Tragedy* (a 'revenge tragedy' and one of the most popular plays of Elizabethan times).	
1590	Spenser's *Faerie Queene* (Books I–III) published.	
1592	Marlowe's *Doctor Faustus* and *Edward II* first staged. Witchcraft trials in Scotland. Robert Greene, a rival playwright, refers to Shakespeare as 'an upstart crow' and 'the only Shake-scene in a country'.	*Titus Andronicus* *Henry VI, Parts I, II and III* *Richard III*
1593	London theatres closed by the plague. Christopher Marlowe killed in a Deptford tavern.	*Two Gentlemen of Verona* *Comedy of Errors* *The Taming of the Shrew* *Love's Labour's Lost*
1594	Shakespeare's company becomes The Lord Chamberlain's Men.	*Romeo and Juliet*

1595	Raleigh's first expedition to Guiana. Last expedition of Drake and Hawkins (both died).	*Richard II* *A Midsummer Night's Dream*
1596	Spenser's *Faerie Queene* (Books IV–VI) published. James Burbage buys rooms at Blackfriars and begins to convert them into a theatre.	*King John* *The Merchant of Venice* Shakespeare's son Hamnet dies. Shakespeare's father is granted a coat of arms.
1597	James Burbage dies, his son Richard, a famous actor, turns the Blackfriars Theatre into a private playhouse.	*Henry IV (Part I)* Shakespeare buys and redecorates New Place at Stratford.
1598	Death of Philip II of Spain	*Henry IV (Part II)* *Much Ado About Nothing*
1599	Death of Edmund Spenser. The Globe Theatre completed at Bankside by Richard and Cuthbert Burbage.	*Henry V* *Julius Caesar* *As You Like It*
1600	Fortune Theatre built at Cripplegate. East India Company founded for the extension of English trade and influence in the East. The Children of the Chapel begin to use the hall at Blackfriars.	*Merry Wives of Windsor* *Troilus and Cressida*
1601		*Hamlet*
1602	Sir Thomas Bodley's library opened at Oxford.	*Twelfth Night*
1603	Death of Queen Elizabeth. James I comes to the throne. Shakespeare's company becomes The King's Men. Raleigh tried, condemned and sent to the Tower	
1604	Treaty of peace with Spain	*Measure for Measure* *Othello* *All's Well that Ends Well*
1605	The Gunpowder Plot: an attempt by a group of Catholics to blow up the Houses of Parliament.	

1606	Guy Fawkes and other plotters executed.	*Macbeth* *King Lear*
1607	Virginia, in America, colonized. A great frost in England.	*Antony and Cleopatra* *Timon of Athens* *Coriolanus* Shakespeare's daughter, Susanna, married to Dr. John Hall.
1608	The company of the Children of the Chapel Royal (who had performed at Blackfriars for ten years) is disbanded. John Milton born. Notorious pirates executed in London.	Richard Burbage leases the Blackfriars Theatre to six of his fellow actors, including Shakespeare. *Pericles, Prince of Tyre*
1609		Shakespeare's Sonnets published.
1610	A great drought in England	*Cymbeline*
1611	Chapman completes his great translation of the *Iliad*, the story of Troy. Authorized Version of the Bible published.	*A Winter's Tale* *The Tempest*
1612	Webster's *The White Devil* first staged.	Shakespeare's brother, Gilbert, dies.
1613	Globe theatre burnt down during a performance of *Henry VIII* (the firing of small cannon set fire to the thatched roof). Webster's *Duchess of Malfi* first staged.	*Henry VIII* *Two Noble Kinsmen* Shakespeare buys a house at Blackfriars.
1614	Globe Theatre rebuilt in 'far finer manner than before'.	
1616	Ben Jonson publishes his plays in one volume. Raleigh released from the Tower in order to prepare an expedition to the gold mines of Guiana.	Shakespeare's daughter, Judith, marries Thomas Quiney. Death of Shakespeare on his birthday, April 23rd.
1618	Raleigh returns to England and is executed on the charge for which he was imprisoned in 1603.	
1623	Publication of the Folio edition of Shakespeare's plays	Death of Anne Shakespeare (née Hathaway).

Life & Times

William Shakespeare the Playwright

There exists a curious paradox when it comes to the life of William Shakespeare. He easily has more words written about him than any other famous English writer, yet we know the least about him. This inevitably means that most of what is written about him is either fabrication or speculation. The reason why so little is known about Shakespeare is that he wasn't a novelist or a historian or a man of letters. He was a playwright, and playwrights were considered fairly low on the social pecking order in Elizabethan society. Writing plays was about providing entertainment for the masses – the great unwashed. It was the equivalent to being a journalist for a tabloid newspaper.

In fact, we only know of Shakespeare's work because two of his friends had the foresight to collect his plays together following his death and have them printed. The only reason they did so was apparently because they rated his talent and thought it would be a shame if his words were lost.

Consequently his body of work has ever since been assessed and reassessed as the greatest contribution to English literature. That is despite the fact that we know that different printers took it upon themselves to heavily edit the material they worked from. We also know that Elizabethan plays were worked and reworked frequently, so that they evolved over time until they were honed to perfection, which means that many different hands played their part in the active writing process. It would therefore be fair to say that any play attributed to Shakespeare is unlikely to contain a great deal of original input. Even the plots were based on well known historical events, so it would be hard to know what fragments of any Shakespeare play came from that single mind.

One might draw a comparison with the Christian bible, which remains such a compelling read because it came from the collaboration of many contributors and translators over centuries, who each adjusted the stories until they could no longer be improved. As virtually nothing is known of Shakespeare's life and even less about his method of working, we shall never know the truth about his plays. They certainly contain some very elegant phrasing, clever plot devices and plenty of words never before seen in print, but as to whether Shakespeare invented them from a unique imagination or whether he simply took them from others around him is anyone's guess.

The best bet seems to be that Shakespeare probably took the lead role in devising the original drafts of the plays, but was open to collaboration from any source when it came to developing them into workable scripts for effective performances. He would have had to work closely with his fellow actors in rehearsals, thereby finding out where to edit, abridge, alter, reword and so on.

In turn, similar adjustments would have occurred in his absence, so that definitive versions of his plays never really existed. In effect Shakespeare was only responsible for providing the framework of plays, upon which others took liberties over time. This wasn't helped by the fact that the English language itself was not definitive at that time either. The consequence was that people took it upon themselves to spell words however they pleased or to completely change words and phrasing to suit their own preferences.

It is easy to see then, that Shakespeare's plays were always going to have lives of their own, mutating and distorting in detail like Chinese whispers. The culture of creative preservation was simply not established in Elizabethan England. Creative ownership of Shakespeare's plays was lost to him as soon as he released them into the consciousness of others. They saw nothing wrong with taking his ideas and running with them, because no one had ever suggested that one shouldn't, and Shakespeare probably regarded his work in the same way. His plays weren't sacrosanct works of art, they were templates for theatre folk to make their livings from, so they had every right to mould them into productions that drew in the crowds as effectively as possible. Shakespeare was like the helmsman of a sailing ship, steering the vessel but wholly reliant on the team work of his crew to arrive at the desired destination.

It seems that Shakespeare certainly had a natural gift, but the genius of his plays may be attributable to the collective efforts of Shakespeare and others. It is a rather satisfying notion to think that *his* plays might actually be the creative outpourings of the Elizabethan milieu in which Shakespeare immersed himself. That makes them important social documents as well as seminal works of the English language.

Money in Shakespeare's Day

It is extremely difficult, if not impossible, to relate the value of money in our time to its value in another age and to compare prices of commodities today and in the past. Many items *are* simply not comparable on grounds of quality or serviceability.

There was a bewildering variety of coins in use in Elizabethan England. As nearly all English and European coins were gold or silver, they had intrinsic value apart from their official value. This meant that foreign coins circulated freely in England and were officially recognized, for example the French crown (écu) worth about 30p (72 cents), and the Spanish ducat worth about 33p (79 cents). The following table shows some of the coins mentioned by Shakespeare and their relation to one another.

GOLD	British	American	SILVER	British	American
sovereign (heavy type)	£1.50	$3.60	shilling	10p	24c
sovereign (light type)	66p–£1	$1.58–$2.40	groat	1.5p	4c
angel					
royal	33p–50p	79c–$1.20			
noble	50p	$1.20			
crown	25p	60c			

A comparison of the following prices in Shakespeare's time with the prices of the same items today will give some idea of the change in the value of money.

ITEM	PRICE British	American	ITEM	PRICE British	American
beef, per lb.	0.5p	1c	cherries (lb.)	1p	2c
mutton, leg	7.5p	18c	7 oranges	1p	2c
rabbit	3.5p	9c	1 lemon	1p	2c
chicken	3p	8c	cream (quart)	2.5p	6c
potatoes (lb)	10p	24c	sugar (lb.)	£1	$2.40
carrots (bunch)	1p	2c	sack (wine) (gallon)	14p	34c
8 artichokes	4p	9c	tobacco (oz.)	25p	60c
1 cucumber	1p	2c	biscuits (lb.)	12.5p	30c

INTRODUCTION

Michael Bogdanov's modern-dress production of *The Taming of the Shrew* in 1979 was well received in terms of its theatrical competence but a number of critics felt that however well done, it had better not been done at all. Michael Billington in the *Guardian* doubted that there was any reason to revive a play 'that seems totally offensive to our age and our society. My own feeling is that it should be put back firmly and squarely on the shelf'. Suggestions of censorship, as it were, have at least the merit of indicating that the offending object is being taken seriously, nor is Billington the first to find *The Shrew* a peculiarly damning blot on Shakespeare's output: Shaw famously registered shame at 'the lord-of-creation moral implied in the wager and the speech put into the woman's own mouth'. *The Shrew* has generally proved a bit of a facer for those who would claim that Shakespeare is a great universal genius with ideas that transcend the limitations of his time. Hence the tendency of modern readings and productions either to imply that Shakespeare did not really acquiesce in the apparent patriarchal assumptions of the taming plot (nor the reductiveness about female charm implied in Bianca's defection from maidenly modesty), or to suggest that even if he did, the usefulness of the play for the twentieth century is to expose the latent misogyny and brutality that still form the real infrastructure of our *bien pensant*, politically correct culture.

One way of distancing Shakespeare from the implications of the taming plot has been to repair the broken frame of the play, increasing the significance of the Sly plot by importing material from the anonymous *The Taming of a Shrew*, printed in 1594 and possibly a 'memorial reconstruction' of a Shakespearean original. The taming and submission of Katherine can then be made to appear an unattainable and possibly rather vulgar male fantasy of domination, a dream of empowerment not unlike the violent fantasies of Pirate Jenny in Brecht's *Threepenny Opera*. Alternatively, the play can be made to appear more coherent by privileging one or other of its generic modes. On the one hand by ignoring the incipient psychological complexity in the treatment of Katherine in particular (she is after all not the favoured child of her father and Bianca's butter-wouldn't-melt-in-her-mouth demeanour might irritate more than a shrew), and taking the whole as a farcical romp with no power to move or upset. On the other side, the farcical nastinesses can be played down in favour of modern notions of relationship where all is fair between the couple because they really love each other, win through to equality within properly constituted hierarchy, and are even, in the most sentimental versions of such a reading, complicit in Kate's response to the wager.

Certainly H. J. Oliver in his introduction to the New Oxford edition of the play feels that Shakespeare's not having provided a generically consistent play is a consequence of his youthfulness when he devised it – it is 'a young dramatist's attempt to mingle two genres that cannot be combined'. But if generic miscegenation is an effect of youth, then it is surprising to find it again in *All's Well That Ends Well* and *Measure for Measure*. Since in these plays it does much to earn the description 'problem plays', it might be well to consider if this is not also the effect in *The Shrew*. The clash of farcical folk-tale in the taming plot with the legitimate desires of both Petruchio and Katherine for lives that they can live, betrays the inconsistences and half-truths that are daily tolerated and evaded. There seems to me no possible way of doubting that Shakespeare presents Katherine's speech of submission to an idealised hierarchy of gender relationships without irony, but he surely does not do so without thought or without demonstrating the worst that can be said about its potential for physical and psychological tyranny.

The rewards for Katherine's submission in life, as it were, are presumably those 'good days and long' that Petruchio has already stated as his goal. Since it comes as a definitive culmination to the action, the audience is left with no sense of need for its endless repetition, it frames a way of life, while shrewishness is on the contrary a lifetime career, the future of Bianca and the widow. This is not modern but it is not too bad in the circumstances. And the reward in the theatre is the complete stage dominance of Kate. It is possible, of course, to pluck weary disaster out of Katherine's eloquent dignity but it seems not worth the trouble.

LIST OF CHARACTERS

A Lord, A Hostess, A Page, Players, Huntsmen, and Servants,
Persons in the Induction

Christopher Sly	a tinker
Baptista Minola	a gentleman of Padua
Vincentio	a merchant of Pisa
Lucentio	son to Vincentio, in love with Bianca
Petruchio	a gentleman of Verona, a suitor to Katherina
Gremio *Hortensio*	} suitors to Bianca
Tranio *Biondello*	} servants to Lucentio
Grumio *Curtis*	} servants to Petruchio
A Pedant	
Katherina the shrew, *Bianca*	} daughters of Baptista

A Tailor, a Haberdasher, and Servants attending on Baptista
and Petruchio

The scene: Padua, and Petruchio's house in the country

INDUCTION
Scene I

Before an alehouse on a heath.

[Enter Hostess and SLY.*]*

Sly

I'll pheeze you, in faith.

Hostess

A pair of stocks, you rogue!

Sly

Y'are a baggage; the Slys are no rogues. Look in the
chronicles: we came in with Richard Conqueror.
Therefore, paucas pallabris; let the world slide. Sessa!   5

Hostess

You will not pay for the glasses you have burst?

Sly

No, not a denier. Go by, Saint Jeronimy, go to thy cold
bed and warm thee.

Hostess

I know my remedy; I must go fetch the thirdborough.

[Exit.]

Sly

Third, or fourth, or fifth borough, I'll answer him by   10
law. I'll not budge an inch, boy; let him come, and
kindly. *[Falls asleep.]*

[Wind horns. Enter a Lord from hunting, with his Train.]

Lord

Huntsman, I charge thee, tender well my hounds;
Brach Merriman, the poor cur, is emboss'd;
And couple Clowder with the deep-mouth'd brach.   15
Saw'st thou not, boy, how Silver made it good
At the hedge corner, in the coldest fault?
I would not lose the dog for twenty pound.

1 Huntsman

    Why, Belman is as good as he, my lord;

20   He cried upon it at the merest loss,

    And twice to-day pick'd out the dullest scent;

    Trust me, I take him for the better dog.

Lord

    Thou art a fool; if Echo were as fleet,

    I would esteem him worth a dozen such.

25   But sup them well, and look unto them all;

    To-morrow I intend to hunt again.

1 Huntsman

    I will, my lord.

Lord

    What's here? One dead, or drunk?

    See, doth he breathe?

2 Huntsman

30   He breathes, my lord. Were he not warm'd with ale,

    This were a bed but cold to sleep so soundly.

Lord

    O monstrous beast, how like a swine he lies!

    Grim death, how foul and loathsome is thine image!

    Sirs, I will practise on this drunken man.

35   What think you, if he were convey'd to bed,

    Wrapp'd in sweet clothes, rings put upon his fingers,

    A most delicious banquet by his bed,

    And brave attendants near him when he wakes,

    Would not the beggar then forget himself?

1 Huntsman

40   Believe me, lord, I think he cannot choose.

2 Huntsman

    It would seem strange unto him when he wak'd.

Lord

    Even as a flatt'ring dream or worthless fancy.

    Then take him up, and manage well the jest:

    Carry him gently to my fairest chamber,

45   And hang it round with all my wanton pictures;

    Balm his foul head in warm distilled waters,

And burn sweet wood to make the lodging sweet;
Procure me music ready when he wakes,
To make a dulcet and a heavenly sound;
And if he chance to speak, be ready straight,   50
And with a low submissive reverence
Say 'What is it your honour will command?'
Let one attend him with a silver basin
Full of rose-water and bestrew'd with flowers;
Another bear the ewer, the third a diaper,   55
And say 'Will't please your lordship cool your hands?'
Some one be ready with a costly suit,
And ask him what apparel he will wear;
Another tell him of his hounds and horse,
And that his lady mourns at his disease;   60
Persuade him that he hath been lunatic,
And, when he says he is, say that he dreams,
For he is nothing but a mighty lord.
This do, and do it kindly, gentle sirs;
It will be pastime passing excellent,   65
If it be husbanded with modesty.

1 *Huntsman*

My lord, I warrant you we will play our part
As he shall think by our true diligence
He is no less than what we say he is.

Lord

Take him up gently, and to bed with him;   70
And each one to his office when he wakes.

[SLY is carried out. A trumpet sounds.]

Sirrah, go see what trumpet 'tis that sounds –

[Exit Servant.]

Belike some noble gentleman that means,
Travelling some journey, to repose him here.

[Re-enter a Servant.]

How now! who is it?

Servant

75   An't please your honour, players
    That offer service to your lordship.

Lord

    Bid them come near.

[Enter Players.]

    Now, fellows, you are welcome.

Players

                      We thank your honour.

Lord

    Do you intend to stay with me to-night?

Player

80   So please your lordship to accept our duty.

Lord

    With all my heart. This fellow I remember
    Since once he play'd a farmer's eldest son;
    'Twas where you woo'd the gentlewoman so well.
    I have forgot your name; but, sure, that part

85   Was aptly fitted and naturally perform'd.

Player

    I think 'twas Soto that your honour means.

Lord

    'Tis very true; thou didst it excellent.
    Well, you are come to me in a happy time,
    The rather for I have some sport in hand

90   Wherein your cunning can assist me much.
    There is a lord will hear you play to-night;
    But I am doubtful of your modesties,
    Lest, over-eying of his odd behaviour,
    For yet his honour never heard a play,

95   You break into some merry passion
    And so offend him; for I tell you, sirs,
    If you should smile, he grows impatient.

Player

    Fear not, my lord; we can contain ourselves,
    Were he the veriest antic in the world.

Lord

    Go, sirrah, take them to the buttery,   100
    And give them friendly welcome every one;
    Let them want nothing that my house affords.

       [Exit one with the Players.]

    Sirrah, go you to Barthol'mew my page,
    And see him dress'd in all suits like a lady;
    That done, conduct him to the drunkard's chamber,   105
    And call him 'madam', do him obeisance.
    Tell him from me – as he will win my love –
    He bear himself with honourable action,
    Such as he hath observ'd in noble ladies
    Unto their lords, by them accomplished;   110
    Such duty to the drunkard let him do,
    With soft low tongue and lowly courtesy,
    And say 'What is't your honour will command,
    Wherein your lady and your humble wife
    May show her duty and make known her love?'   115
    And then with kind embracements, tempting kisses,
    And with declining head into his bosom,
    Bid him shed tears, as being overjoyed
    To see her noble lord restor'd to health,
    Who for this seven years hath esteemed him   120
    No better than a poor and loathsome beggar.
    And if the boy have not a woman's gift
    To rain a shower of commanded tears,
    An onion will do well for such a shift,
    Which, in a napkin being close convey'd   125
    Shall in despite enforce a watery eye.
    See this dispatch'd with all the haste thou canst;
    Anon I'll give thee more instructions.

       [Exit a Servant.]

    I know the boy will well usurp the grace,
    Voice, gait, and action, of a gentlewoman;   130
    I long to hear him call the drunkard 'husband';

And how my men will stay themselves from laughter
When they do homage to this simple peasant.
I'll in to counsel them; haply my presence
135   May well abate the over-merry spleen,
Which otherwise would grow into extremes.

[Exeunt.]

Scene II

_____

A bedchamber in the Lord's house.

[Enter aloft SLY, with Attendants; some with apparel, basin and ewer, and other appurtenances; and Lord.]

Sly

    For God's sake, a pot of small ale.

1 Servant

    Will't please your lordship drink a cup of sack?

2 Servant

    Will't please your honour taste of these conserves?

3 Servant

    What raiment will your honour wear to-day?

Sly

    I am Christophero Sly; call not me 'honour' nor   5
'lordship'. I ne'er drank sack in my life; and if you give
me any conserves, give me conserves of beef. Ne'er ask
me what raiment I'll wear, for I have no more doublets
than backs, no more stockings than legs, nor no more
shoes than feet – nay, sometime more feet than shoes,   10
or such shoes as my toes look through the overleather.

Lord

    Heaven cease this idle humour in your honour!
O, that a mighty man of such descent,
Of such possessions, and so high esteem,
Should be infused with so foul a spirit!   15

Sly

    What, would you make me mad? Am not I Christopher
Sly, old Sly's son of Burton Heath; by birth a pedlar, by
education a cardmaker, by transmutation a bearherd,
and now by present profession a tinker? Ask Marian
Hacket, the fat alewife of Wincot, if she know me not;   20
if she say I am not fourteen pence on the score for sheer
ale, score me up for the lying'st knave in Christendom.
What! I am not bestraught.

[Taking a pot of ale]

Here's –
3 Servant
25   O, this it is that makes your lady mourn!
2 Servant
O, this is it that makes your servants droop!
Lord
Hence comes it that your kindred shuns your house,
As beaten hence by your strange lunacy.
O noble lord, bethink thee of thy birth!
30   Call home thy ancient thoughts from banishment,
And banish hence these abject lowly dreams.
Look how thy servants do attend on thee,
Each in his office ready at thy beck.
Wilt thou have music? Hark! Apollo plays,

[Music.]

35   And twenty caged nightingales do sing.
Or wilt thou sleep? We'll have thee to a couch
Softer and sweeter than the lustful bed
On purpose trimm'd up for Semiramis.
Say thou wilt walk: we will bestrew the ground.
40   Or wilt thou ride? Thy horses shall be trapp'd,
Their harness studded all with gold and pearl.
Dost thou love hawking? Thou hast hawks will soar
Above the morning lark. Or wilt thou hunt?
Thy hounds shall make the welkin answer them
45   And fetch shrill echoes from the hollow earth.
1 Servant
Say thou wilt course; thy grey-hounds are as swift
As breathed stags; ay, fleeter than the roe.
2 Servant
Dost thou love pictures? We will fetch thee straight
Adonis painted by a running brook,
50   And Cytherea all in sedges hid,
Which seem to move and wanton with her breath
Even as the waving sedges play wi' th' wind.

Lord

We'll show thee Io as she was a maid
And how she was beguiled and surpris'd,
As lively painted as the deed was done.   55

3 Servant

Or Daphne roaming through a thorny wood,
Scratching her legs, that one shall swear she bleeds;
And at that sight shall sad Apollo weep,
So workmanly the blood and tears are drawn.

Lord

Thou art a lord, and nothing but a lord.   60
Thou hast a lady far more beautiful
Than any woman in this waning age.

1 Servant

And, till the tears that she hath shed for thee
Like envious floods o'er-run her lovely face,
She was the fairest creature in the world;   65
And yet she is inferior to none.

Sly

Am I a lord and have I such a lady?
Or do I dream? Or have I dream'd till now?
I do not sleep: I see, I hear, I speak;
I smell sweet savours, and I feel soft things.   70
Upon my life, I am a lord indeed,
And not a tinker, nor Christopher Sly.
Well, bring our lady hither to our sight;
And once again, a pot o' th' smallest ale.

2 Servant

Will't please your Mightiness to wash your hands?   75
O, how we joy to see your wit restor'd!
O, that once more you knew but what you are!
These fifteen years you have been in a dream;
Or, when you wak'd, so wak'd as if you slept.

Sly

These fifteen years! by my fay, a goodly nap.   80
But did I never speak of all that time?

1 Servant

> O, yes, my lord, but very idle words;
> For though you lay here in this goodly chamber,
> Yet would you say ye were beaten out of door;
85 And rail upon the hostess of the house,
> And say you would present her at the leet,
> Because she brought stone jugs and no seal'd quarts.
> Sometimes you would call out for Cicely Hacket.

Sly

> Ay, the woman's maid of the house.

3 Servant

90 Why, sir, you know no house nor no such maid,
> Nor no such men as you have reckon'd up,
> As Stephen Sly, and old John Naps of Greece,
> And Peter Turph, and Henry Pimpernell;
> And twenty more such names and men as these,
95 Which never were, nor no man ever saw.

Sly

> Now, Lord be thanked for my good amends!

All

> Amen.

[Enter the Page as a lady, with Attendants.]

Sly

> I thank thee; thou shalt not lose by it.

Page

> How fares my noble lord?

Sly

100 Marry, I fare well; for here is cheer enough.
> Where is my wife?

Page

> Here, noble lord; what is thy will with her?

Sly

> Are you my wife, and will not call me husband?
> My men should call me 'lord'; I am your goodman.

Page

105 My husband and my lord, my lord and husband;
> I am your wife in all obedience.

Sly

    I know it well. What must I call her?

Lord

                                    Madam.

Sly

    Al'ce madam, or Joan madam?

Lord

    Madam, and nothing else; so lords call ladies.

Sly

    Madam wife, they say that I have dream'd   110
    And slept above some fifteen year or more.

Page

    Ay, and the time seems thirty unto me,
    Being all this time abandon'd from your bed.

Sly

    'Tis much. Servants, leave me and her alone.

[Exeunt Servants.]

    Madam, undress you, and come now to bed.   115

Page

    Thrice noble lord, let me entreat of you
    To pardon me yet for a night or two;
    Or, if not so, until the sun be set.
    For your physicians have expressly charg'd,
    In peril to incur your former malady,   120
    That I should yet absent me from your bed.
    I hope this reason stands for my excuse.

Sly

    Ay, it stands so that I may hardly tarry so long. But
    I would be loath to fall into my dreams again. I will
    therefore tarry in despite of the flesh and the blood.   125

[Enter a Messenger.]

Messenger

    You honour's players, hearing your amendment,
    Are come to play a pleasant comedy;
    For so your doctors hold it very meet,
    Seeing too much sadness hath congeal'd your blood,

130   And melancholy is the nurse of frenzy.
       Therefore they thought it good you hear a play
       And frame your mind to mirth and merriment,
       Which bars a thousand harms and lengthens life.

Sly

       Marry, I will; let them play it. Is not a comonty a
135   Christmas gambold or a tumbling-trick?

Page

       No, my good lord, it is more pleasing stuff.

Sly

       What, household stuff?

Page

       It is a kind of history.

Sly

       Well, we'll see't. Come, madam wife, sit by my side and
140   let the world slip; we shall ne'er be younger.

[They sit down.]

[A flourish of trumpets announces the play.]

ACT ONE
Scene I

Padua. A public place.

[Enter LUCENTIO *and his man* TRANIO.*]*

Lucentio
>Tranio, since for the great desire I had
>To see fair Padua, nursery of arts,
>I am arriv'd for fruitful Lombardy,
>The pleasant garden of great Italy,
>And by my father's love and leave am arm'd   5
>With his good will and thy good company,
>My trusty servant well approv'd in all,
>Here let us breathe, and haply institute
>A course of learning and ingenious studies.
>Pisa, renowned for grave citizens,   10
>Gave me my being and my father first,
>A merchant of great traffic through the world,
>Vincentio, come of the Bentivolii;
>Vincentio's son, brought up in Florence,
>It shall become to serve all hopes conceiv'd,   15
>To deck his fortune with his virtuous deeds.
>And therefore, Tranio, for the time I study,
>Virtue and that part of philosophy
>Will I apply that treats of happiness
>By virtue specially to be achiev'd.   20
>Tell me thy mind; for I have Pisa left
>And am to Padua come as he that leaves
>A shallow plash to plunge him in the deep,
>And with satiety seeks to quench his thirst.
Tranio
>Mi perdonato, gentle master mine;   25
>I am in all affected as yourself;
>Glad that you thus continue your resolve

To suck the sweets of sweet philosophy.
Only, good master, while we do admire
30   This virtue and this moral discipline,
Let's be no Stoics nor no stocks, I pray,
Or so devote to Aristotle's checks
As Ovid be an outcast quite abjur'd.
Balk logic with acquaintance that you have,
35   And practise rhetoric in your common talk;
Music and poesy use to quicken you;
The mathematics and the metaphysics,
Fall to them as you find your stomach serves you.
No profit grows where is no pleasure ta'en;
40   In brief, sir, study what you most affect.
Lucentio
Gramercies, Tranio, well dost thou advise.
If, Biondello, thou wert come ashore,
We could at once put us in readiness,
And take a lodging fit to entertain
45   Such friends as time in Padua shall beget.

[*Enter* BAPTISTA *with his two daughters,* KATHERINA
and BIANCA; GREMIO, *a pantaloon,* HORTENSIO, *suitor
to Bianca.* LUCENTIO *and* TRANIO *stand by.*]

But stay awhile; what company is this?
Tranio
Master, some show to welcome us to town.
Baptista
Gentlemen, importune me no farther,
For how I firmly am resolv'd you know;
50   That is, not to bestow my youngest daughter
Before I have a husband for the elder.
If either of you both love Katherina,
Because I know you well and love you well,
Leave shall you have to court her at your pleasure.
Gremio
55   To cart her rather. She's too rough for me.
There, there, Hortensio, will you any wife?

Katherina

   [To BAPTISTA*]* I pray you, sir, is it your will

   To make a stale of me amongst these mates?

Hortensio

   Mates, maid! How mean you that? No mates for you,

   Unless you were of gentler, milder mould.   60

Katherina

   I' faith, sir, you shall never need to fear;

   Iwis it is not halfway to her heart;

   But if it were, doubt not her care should be

   To comb your noddle with a three-legg'd stool,

   And paint your face, and use you like a fool.   65

Hortensio

   From all such devils, good Lord deliver us!

Gremio

   And me, too, good Lord!

Tranio

   Husht, master! Here's some good pastime toward;

   That wench is stark mad or wonderful froward.

Lucentio

   But in the other's silence do I see   70

   Maid's mild behaviour and sobriety.

   Peace, Tranio!

Tranio

   Well said, master; mum! and gaze your fill.

Baptista

   Gentlemen, that I may soon make good

   What I have said – Bianca, get you in;   75

   And let it not displease thee, good Bianca,

   For I will love thee ne'er the less, my girl.

Katherina

   A pretty peat! it is best

   Put finger in the eye, an she knew why.

Bianca

   Sister, content you in my discontent.   80

   Sir, to your pleasure humbly I subscribe;

   My books and instruments shall be my company,

   On them to look, and practise by myself.

Lucentio
Hark, Tranio, thou mayst hear Minerva speak!

Hortensio
85 Signior Baptista, will you be so strange?
Sorry am I that our good will effects
Bianca's grief.

Gremio
                              Why will you mew her up,
Signior Baptista, for this fiend of hell,
And make her bear the penance of her tongue?

Baptista
90 Gentlemen, content ye; I am resolv'd.
Go in, Bianca.   *[Exit* BIANCA.*]*
And for I know she taketh most delight
In music, instruments, and poetry,
Schoolmasters will I keep within my house
95 Fit to instruct her youth. If you, Hortensio,
Or, Signior Gremio, you, know any such,
Prefer them hither; for to cunning men
I will be very kind, and liberal
To mine own children in good bringing-up;
100 And so, farewell. Katherina, you may stay;
For I have more to commune with Bianca. *[Exit.]*

Katherina
Why, and I trust I may go too, may I not?
What! shall I be appointed hours, as though, belike,
I knew not what to take and what to leave? Ha!

[Exit.]

Gremio
105 You may go to the devil's dam; your gifts are so good
here's none will hold you. There! Love is not so great,
Hortensio, but we may blow our nails together, and fast
it fairly out; our cake's dough on both sides. Farewell;
yet, for the love I bear my sweet Bianca, if I can by any
110 means light on a fit man to teach her that wherein she
delights, I will wish him to her father.

Hortensio
So will I, Signior Gremio; but a word, I pray. Though
the nature of our quarrel yet never brook'd parle, know
now, upon advice, it toucheth us both – that we may
yet again have access to our fair mistress, and be happy 115
rivals in Bianca's love – to labour and effect one thing
specially.

Gremio
What's that, I pray?

Hortensio
Marry, sir, to get a husband for her sister.

Gremio
A husband? a devil.   120

Hortensio
I say a husband.

Gremio
I say a devil. Think'st thou, Hortensio, though her
father be very rich, any man is so very a fool to be
married to hell?

Hortensio
Tush, Gremio! Though it pass your patience and mine 125
to endure her loud alarums, why, man, there be good
fellows in the world, an a man could light on them,
would take her with all faults, and money enough.

Gremio
I cannot tell; but I had as lief take her dowry with
this condition – to be whipp'd at the high cross every 130
morning.

Hortensio
Faith, as you say, there's small choice in rotten apples.
But, come; since this bar in law makes us friends, it
shall be so far forth friendly maintain'd till by helping
Baptista's eldest daughter to a husband we set his 135
youngest free for a husband, and then have to't afresh.
Sweet Bianca! Happy man be his dole! He that runs
fastest gets the ring. How say you, Signior Gremio?

Gremio

I am agreed; and would I had given him the best horse
140   in Padua to begin his wooing that would thoroughly
woo her, wed her, and bed her, and rid the house of
her! Come on.

[Exeunt GREMIO *and* HORTENSIO.*]*

Tranio

I pray, sir, tell me, is it possible
That love should of a sudden take such hold?

Lucentio

145   O Tranio, till I found it to be true,
I never thought it possible or likely.
But see! while idly I stood looking on,
I found the effect of love in idleness;
And now in plainness do confess to thee,
150   That art to me as secret and as dear
As Anna to the Queen of Carthage was –
Tranio, I burn, I pine, I perish, Tranio,
If I achieve not this young modest girl.
Counsel me, Tranio, for I know thou canst;
155   Assist me, Tranio, for I know thou wilt.

Tranio

Master, it is no time to chide you now;
Affection is not rated from the heart;
If love have touch'd you, nought remains but so:
'Redime te captum quam queas minimo'.

Lucentio

160   Gramercies, lad. Go forward; this contents;
The rest will comfort, for thy counsel's sound.

Tranio

Master, you look'd so longly on the maid,
Perhaps you mark'd not what's the pith of all,

Lucentio

O, yes, I saw sweet beauty in her face,
165   Such as the daughter of Agenor had,
That made great Jove to humble him to her hand,
When with his knees he kiss'd the Cretan strand.

Tranio

Saw you no more? Mark'd you not how her sister
Began to scold and raise up such a storm
That mortal ears might hardly endure the din?   170

Lucentio

Tranio, I saw her coral lips to move,
And with her breath she did perfume the air;
Sacred and sweet was all I saw in her.

Tranio

Nay, then 'tis time to stir him from his trance.
I pray, awake, sir. If you love the maid,   175
Bend thoughts and wits to achieve her. Thus it stands:
Her elder sister is so curst and shrewd
That, till the father rid his hands of her,
Master, your love must live a maid at home;
And therefore has he closely mew'd her up,   180
Because she will not be annoy'd with suitors.

Lucentio

Ah, Tranio, what a cruel father's he!
But art thou not advis'd he took some care
To get her cunning schoolmasters to instruct her?

Tranio

Ay, marry, am I, sir, and now 'tis plotted.   185

Lucentio

I have it, Tranio.

Tranio

               Master, for my hand,
Both our inventions meet and jump in one.

Lucentio

Tell me thine first.

Tranio

               You will be schoolmaster,
And undertake the teaching of the maid –
That's your device.

Lucentio

               It is. May it be done?   190

Tranio

Not possible; for who shall bear your part

And be in Padua here Vincentio's son;
Keep house and ply his book, welcome his friends,
Visit his countrymen, and banquet them?

Lucentio

195   Basta, content thee, for I have it full.
We have not yet been seen in any house,
Nor we can be distinguish'd by our faces
For man or master. Then it follows thus:
Thou shall be master, Tranio, in my stead,
200   Keep house and port and servants, as I should;
I will some other be – some Florentine,
Some Neapolitan, or meaner man of Pisa.
'Tis hatch'd, and shall be so. Tranio, at once
Uncase thee; take my colour'd hat and cloak.
205   When Biondello comes, he waits on thee;
But I will charm him first to keep his tongue.

Tranio

So had you need.

[They exchange habits.]

In brief, sir, sith it your pleasure is,
And I am tied to be obedient –
210   For so your father charg'd me at our parting:
'Be serviceable to my son' quoth he,
Although I think 'twas in another sense –
I am content to be Lucentio,
Because so well I love Lucentio.

Lucentio

215   Tranio, be so because Lucentio loves;
And let me be a slave t' achieve that maid
Whose sudden sight hath thrall'd my wounded eye.

[Enter BIONDELLO.]

Here comes the rogue. Sirrah, where have you been?

Biondello

Where have I been! Nay, how now! where are you?
220   Master, has my fellow Tranio stol'n your clothes?
Or you stol'n his? or both? Pray, what's the news?

Lucentio

    Sirrah, come hither; 'tis no time to jest,

    And therefore frame your manners to the time.

    Your fellow Tranio here, to save my life,

    Puts my apparel and my count'nance on,   225

    And I for my escape have put on his;

    For in a quarrel since I came ashore

    I kill'd a man, and fear I was descried.

    Wait you on him, I charge you, as becomes,

    While I make way from hence to save my life.   230

    You understand me?

Biondello

                 I, sir? Ne'er a whit.

Lucentio

    And not a jot of Tranio in your mouth:

    Tranio is chang'd into Lucentio.

Biondello

    The better for him; would I were so too!

Tranio

    So could I, faith, boy, to have the next wish after,   235

    That Lucentio indeed had Baptista's youngest

        daughter.

    But, sirrah, not for my sake but your master's, I advise

    You use your manners discreetly in all kind of

        companies.

    When I am alone, why, then I am Tranio;

    But in all places else your master Lucentio.   240

Lucentio

    Tranio, let's go.

    One thing more rests, that thyself execute –

    To make one among these wooers. If thou ask me

        why –

    Sufficeth, my reasons are both good and weighty.

                              [Exeunt.]

        [The Presenters above speak.]

1 Servant

245   My lord, you nod; you do not mind the play.

Sly

    Yes, by Saint Anne do I. A good matter, surely; comes
        there any more of it?

Page

    My lord, 'tis but begun.

Sly

    'Tis a very excellent piece of work, madam lady.
        Would 'twere done!

[They sit and mark.]

Scene II

Padua. Before Hortensio's house.

[Enter PETRUCHIO and his man GRUMIO.]

Petruchio
    Verona, for a while I take my leave,
    To see my friends in Padua; but of all
    My best beloved and approved friend,
    Hortensio; and I trow this is his house.
    Here, sirrah Grumio, knock, I say.   5

Grumio
    Knock, sir! Whom should I knock? Is there any man
    has rebus'd your worship?

Petruchio
    Villain, I say, knock me here soundly.

Grumio
    Knock you here, sir? Why, sir, what am I, sir, that I
    should knock you here, sir?   10

Petruchio
    Villain, I say, knock me at this gate,
    And rap we well, or I'll knock your knave's pate.

Grumio
    My master is grown quarrelsome. I should knock you
        first,
    And then I know after who comes by the worst.

Petruchio
    Will it not be?   15
    Faith, sirrah, an you'll not knock I'll ring it;
    I'll try how you can sol-fa, and sing it.

[He wrings him by the ears.]

Grumio
    Help, masters, help! My master is mad.

Petruchio
    Now knock when I bid you, sirrah villain!

[Enter HORTENSIO.*]*

Hortensio

20   How now! what's the matter? My old friend Grumio
      and my good friend Petruchio!
      How do you all at Verona?

Petruchio

      Signior Hortensio, come you to part the fray?
      'Con tutto il cuore ben trovato' may I say.

Hortensio

25   Alla nostra casa ben venuto,
      Molto honorato signor mio Petrucio.
      Rise, Grumio, rise; we will compound this quarrel.

Grumio

      Nay, 'tis no matter, sir, what he 'leges in Latin. If this
      be not a lawful cause for me to leave his service – look

30   you, sir: he bid me knock him and rap him soundly, sir.
      Well, was it fit for a servant to use his master so; being,
      perhaps, for aught I see, two and thirty, a pip out?
      Whom would to God I had well knock'd at first,
      Then had not Grumio come by the worst.

Petruchio

35   A senseless villain! Good Hortensio,
      I bade the rascal knock upon your gate,
      And could not get him for my heart to do it.

Grumio

      Knock at the gate? O heavens! Spake you not these
      words plain: 'Sirrah knock me here, rap me here, knock

40   me well, and knock me soundly'? And come you now
      with 'knocking at the gate'?

Petruchio

      Sirrah, be gone, or talk not, I advise you.

Hortensio

      Petruchio, patience; I am Grumio's pledge;
      Why, this's a heavy chance 'twixt him and you,

45   Your ancient, trusty, pleasant servant Grumio.
      And tell me now, sweet friend, what happy gale
      Blows you to Padua here from old Verona?

Petruchio

Such wind as scatters young men through the world
To seek their fortunes farther than at home,
Where small experience grows. But in a few,   50
Signior Hortensio, thus it stands with me:
Antonio, my father, is deceas'd,
And I have thrust myself into this maze,
Haply to wive and thrive as best I may;
Crowns in my purse I have, and goods at home,   55
And so am come abroad to see the world.

Hortensio

Petruchio, shall I then come roundly to thee
And wish thee to a shrewd ill-favour'd wife?
Thou'dst thank me but a little for my counsel,
And yet I'll promise thee she shall be rich,   60
And very rich; but th'art too much my friend,
And I'll not wish thee to her.

Petruchio

Signior Hortensio, 'twixt such friends as we
Few words suffice; and therefore, if thou know
One rich enough to be Petruchio's wife,   65
As wealth is burden of my wooing dance,
Be she as foul as was Florentius' love,
As old as Sibyl, and as curst and shrewd
As Socrates' Xanthippe or a worse –
She moves me not, or not removes, at least,   70
Affection's edge in me, were she as rough
As are the swelling Adriatic seas.
I come to wive it wealthily in Padua;
If wealthily, then happily in Padua.

Grumio

Nay, look you, sir, he tells you flatly what his mind is.   75
Why, give him gold enough and marry him to a puppet
or an aglet-baby, or an old trot with ne'er a tooth in
her head, though she have as many diseases as two
and fifty horses. Why, nothing comes amiss, so money
comes withal.   80

Hortensio
> Petruchio, since we are stepp'd thus far in,
> I will continue that I broach'd in jest.
> I can, Petruchio, help thee to a wife
> With wealth enough, and young and beauteous;
85   Brought up as best becomes a gentlewoman;
> Her only fault, and that is faults enough,
> Is – that she is intolerable curst,
> And shrewd and froward so beyond all measure
> That, were my state far worser than it is,
90   I would not wed her for a mine of gold.

Petruchio
> Hortensio, peace! thou know'st not gold's effect.
> Tell me her father's name, and 'tis enough;
> For I will board her though she chide as loud
> As thunder when the clouds in autumn crack.

Hortensio
95   Her father is Baptista Minola,
> An affable and courteous gentleman;
> Her name is Katherina Minola,
> Renown'd in Padua for her scolding tongue.

Petruchio
> I know her father, though I know not her;
100 And he knew my deceased father well.
> I will not sleep, Hortensio, till I see her;
> And therefore let me be thus bold with you
> To give you over at this first encounter,
> Unless you will accompany me thither.

Grumio
105 I pray you, sir, let him go while the humour lasts. O'
> my word, an she knew him as well as I do, she would
> think scolding would do little good upon him. She may
> perhaps call him half a score knaves or so. Why, that's
> nothing; an he begin once, he'll rail in his rope-tricks.
110 I'll tell you what, sir: an she stand him but a little, he
> will throw a figure in her face, and so disfigure her with
> it that she shall have no more eyes to see withal than a
> cat. You know him not, sir.

Hortensio

Tarry, Petruchio, I must go with thee,
For in Baptista's keep my treasure is.   115
He hath the jewel of my life in hold,
His youngest daughter, beautiful Bianca;
And her withholds from me, and other more,
Suitors to her and rivals in my love;
Supposing it a thing impossible –   120
For those defects I have before rehears'd –
That ever Katherina will be woo'd.
Therefore this order hath Baptista ta'en,
That none shall have access unto Bianca
Till Katherine the curst have got a husband.   125

Grumio

Katherine the curst!
A title for a maid of all titles the worst.

Hortensio

Now shall my friend Petruchio do me grace,
And offer me disguis'd in sober robes
To old Baptista as a schoolmaster   130
Well seen in music, to instruct Bianca;
That so I may by this device at least
Have leave and leisure to make love to her,
And unsuspected court her by herself.

[Enter GREMIO *with* LUCENTIO *disguised as Cambio.]*

Grumio

Here's no knavery! See, to beguile the old folks, how the 135
young folks lay their heads together! Master, master,
look about you. Who goes there, ha?

Hortensio

Peace, Grumio! It is the rival of my love. Petruchio,
stand by awhile.

Grumio

A proper stripling, and an amorous!   140

[They stand aside.]

Gremio

    O, very well; I have perus'd the note.

    Hark you, sir; I'll have them very fairly bound –

    All books of love, see that at any hand;

    And see you read no other lectures to her.

145   You understand me – over and beside

    Signior Baptista's liberality,

    I'll mend it with a largess. Take your paper too,

    And let me have them very well perfum'd;

    For she is sweeter than perfume itself

150   To whom they go to. What will you read to her?

Lucentio

    Whate'er I read to her, I'll plead for you

    As for my patron, stand you so assur'd,

    As firmly as yourself were still in place;

    Yea, and perhaps with more successful words

155   Than you, unless you were a scholar, sir.

Gremio

    O this learning, what a thing it is!

Grumio

    O this woodcock, what an ass it is!

Petruchio

    Peace, sirrah!

Hortensio

    Grumio, mum! *[Coming forward]* God save you, Signior
        Gremio!

Gremio

160   And you are well met, Signior Hortensio.

    Trow you whither I am going? To Baptista Minola.

    I promis'd to enquire carefully

    About a schoolmaster for the fair Bianca;

    And by good fortune I have lighted well

165   On this young man; for learning and behaviour

    Fit for her turn, well read in poetry

    And other books – good ones, I warrant ye.

Hortensio

    'Tis well; and I have met a gentleman

Hath promis'd me to help me to another,
A fine musician to instruct our mistress;   170
So shall I no whit be behind in duty
To fair Bianca, so beloved of me.

Gremio
Beloved of me – and that my deeds shall prove.

Grumio
And that his bags shall prove.

Hortensio
Gremio, 'tis now no time to vent our love.   175
Listen to me, and if you speak me fair
I'll tell you news indifferent good for either.
Here is a gentleman whom by chance I met,
Upon agreement from us to his liking,
Will undertake to woo curst Katherine;   180
Yea, and to marry her, if her dowry please.

Gremio
So said, so done, is well.
Hortensio, have you told him all her faults?

Petruchio
I know she is an irksome brawling scold;
If that be all, masters, I hear no harm.   185

Gremio
No, say'st me so, friend? What countryman?

Petruchio
Born in Verona, old Antonio's son.
My father dead, my fortune lives for me;
And I do hope good days and long to see.

Gremio
O sir, such a life with such a wife were strange!   190
But if you have a stomach, to't a God's name;
You shall have me assisting you in all.
But will you woo this wild-cat?

Petruchio
                                          Will I live?

Grumio
Will he woo her? Ay, or I'll hang her.

Petruchio

195   Why came I hither but to that intent?
     Think you a little din can daunt mine ears?
     Have I not in my time heard lions roar?
     Have I not heard the sea, puff'd up with winds,
     Rage like an angry boar chafed with sweat?
200   Have I not heard great ordnance in the field,
     And heaven's artillery thunder in the skies?
     Have I not in a pitched battle heard
     Loud 'larums, neighing steeds, and trumpets' clang?
     And do you tell me of a woman's tongue,
205   That gives not half so great a blow to hear
     As will a chestnut in a farmer's fire?
     Tush! tush! fear boys with bugs.

Grumio

                          For he fears none.

Gremio

     Hortensio, hark:
     This gentleman is happily arriv'd
210   My mind presumes, for his own good and ours.

Hortensio

     I promis'd we would be contributors
     And bear his charge of wooing, whatsoe'er.

Gremio

     And so we will – provided that he win her.

Grumio

     I would I were as sure of a good dinner.

    [Enter TRANIO, *bravely apparelled as* LUCENTIO, *and*
                         BIONDELLO.*]*

Tranio

215   Gentlemen, God save you! If I may be bold,
     Tell me, I beseech you, which is the readiest way
     To the house of Signior Baptista Minola?

Biondello

     He that has the two fair daughters; is't he you mean?

Tranio
    Even he, Biondello.
Gremio
    Hark you, sir, you mean not her to –   220
Tranio
    Perhaps him and her, sir; what have you to do?
Petruchio
    Not her that chides, sir, at any hand, I pray.
Tranio
    I love no chiders, sir. Biondello, let's away.
Lucentio
    [Aside] Well begun, Tranio.
Hortensio
                            Sir, a word ere you go.
    Are you a suitor to the maid you talk of, yea or no?   225
Tranio
    And if I be, sir, is it any offence?
Gremio
    No; if without more words you will get you hence.
Tranio
    Why, sir, I pray, are not the streets as free
    For me as for you?
Gremio
                        But so is not she.
Tranio
    For what reason, I beseech you?
Gremio
                            For this reason, if you'll know,   230
    That she's the choice love of Signior Gremio.
Hortensio
    That she's the chosen of Signior Hortensio.
Tranio
    Softly, my masters! If you be gentlemen,
    Do me this right – hear me with patience.
    Baptista is a noble gentleman,   235
    To whom my father is not all unknown,
    And, were his daughter fairer than she is,

She may more suitors have, and me for one.
Fair Leda's daughter had a thousand wooers;
240   Then well one more may fair Bianca have;
And so she shall: Lucentio shall make one,
Though Paris came in hope to speed alone.

Gremio
What, this gentleman will out-talk us all!

Lucentio
Sir, give him head; I know he'll prove a jade.

Petruchio
245   Hortensio, to what end are all these words?

Hortensio
Sir, let me be so bold as ask you,
Did you yet ever see Baptista's daughter?

Tranio
No, sir, but hear I do that he hath two:
The one as famous for a scolding tongue
250   As is the other for beauteous modesty.

Petruchio
Sir, sir, the first's for me; let her go by.

Gremio
Yea, leave that labour to great Hercules,
And let it be more than Alcides' twelve.

Petruchio
Sir, understand you this of me, in sooth:
255   The youngest daughter, whom you hearken for,
Her father keeps from all access of suitors,
And will not promise her to any man
Until the elder sister first be wed.
The younger then is free, and not before.

Tranio
260   If it be so, sir, that you are the man
Must stead us all, and me amongst the rest;
And if you break the ice, and do this feat,
Achieve the elder, set the younger free
For our access – whose hap shall be to have her
265   Will not so graceless be to be ingrate.

Hortensio
    Sir, you say well, and well you do conceive;
    And since you do profess to be a suitor,
    You must, as we do, gratify this gentleman,
    To whom we all rest generally beholding.
Tranio
    Sir, I shall not be slack; in sign whereof,   270
    Please ye we may contrive this afternoon,
    And quaff carouses to our mistress' health;
    And do as adversaries do in law –
    Strive mightily, but eat and drink as friends.
Grumio, Biondello
    O excellent motion! Fellows, let's be gone.   275
Hortensio
    The motion's good indeed, and be it so.
    Petruchio, I shall be your ben venuto.

                        [Exeunt.]

ACT TWO
Scene I

Padua. Baptista's house.

[Enter KATHERINA *and* BIANCA.]

Bianca
> Good sister, wrong me not, nor wrong yourself,
> To make a bondmaid and a slave of me –
> That I disdain; but for these other gawds,
> Unbind my hands, I'll pull them off myself,
5 > Yea, all my raiment, to my petticoat;
> Or what you will command me will I do,
> So well I know my duty to my elders.

Katherina
> Of all thy suitors here I charge thee tell
> Whom thou lov'st best. See thou dissemble not.

Bianca
10 > Believe me, sister, of all the men alive
> I never yet beheld that special face
> Which I could fancy more than any other.

Katherina
> Minion, thou liest. Is't not Hortensio?

Bianca
> If you affect him, sister, here I swear
15 > I'll plead for you myself but you shall have him.

Katherina
> O then, belike, you fancy riches more:
> You will have Gremio to keep you fair.

Bianca
> Is it for him you do envy me so?
> Nay, then you jest; and now I well perceive
20 > You have but jested with me all this while.
> I prithee, sister Kate, untie my hands.

Katherina
    [Strikes her] If that be jest, then all the rest was so.

                    [Enter BAPTISTA.*]*

Baptista
    Why, how now, dame! Whence grows this insolence?
    Bianca, stand aside – poor girl! she weeps.

                    [He unbinds her.]

    Go ply thy needle; meddle not with her.   25
    For shame, thou hilding of a devilish spirit,
    Why dost thou wrong her that did ne'er wrong thee?
    When did she cross thee with a bitter word?
Katherina
    Her silence flouts me, and I'll be reveng'd.

                    [Flies after BIANCA.*]*

Baptista
    What, in my sight? Bianca, get thee in.   30

                    [Exit BIANCA.*]*

Katherina
    What, will you not suffer me? Nay, now I see
    She is your treasure, she must have a husband;
    I must dance bare-foot on her wedding-day,
    And for your love to her lead apes in hell.
    Talk not to me; I will go sit and weep,   35
    Till I can find occasion of revenge.

                    [Exit KATHERINA.*]*

Baptista
    Was ever gentleman thus griev'd as I?
    But who comes here?

    [Enter GREMIO, *with* LUCENTIO *in the habit of a mean
    man;* PETRUCHIO, *with* HORTENSIO *as a musician; and*
    TRANIO, *as Lucentio, with his boy,* BIONDELLO, *bearing
    a lute and books.]*

Gremio
　　Good morrow, neighbour Baptista.
Baptista
40　Good morrow, neighbour Gremio.
　　God save you, gentlemen!
Petruchio
　　And you, good sir! Pray, have you not a daughter
　　Call'd Katherina, fair and virtuous?
Baptista
　　I have a daughter, sir, call'd Katherina.
Gremio
45　You are too blunt; go to it orderly.
Petruchio
　　You wrong me, Signior Gremio; give me leave.
　　I am a gentleman of Verona, sir,
　　That, hearing of her beauty and her wit,
　　Her affability and bashful modesty,
50　Her wondrous qualities and mild behaviour,
　　Am bold to show myself a forward guest
　　Within your house, to make mine eye the witness
　　Of that report which I so oft have heard.
　　And, for an entrance to my entertainment,
55　I do present you with a man of mine,

[Presenting HORTENSIO.*]*

　　Cunning in music and the mathematics,
　　To instruct her fully in those sciences,
　　Whereof I know she is not ignorant.
　　Accept of him, or else you do me wrong –
60　His name is Licio, born in Mantua.
Baptista
　　Y'are welcome, sir, and he for your good sake;
　　But for my daughter Katherine, this I know,
　　She is not for your turn, the more my grief.
Petruchio
　　I see you do not mean to part with her;
65　Or else you like not of my company.

Baptista

 Mistake me not; I speak but as I find.

 Whence are you, sir? What may I call your name?

Petruchio

 Petruchio is my name, Antonio's son,

 A man well known throughout all Italy.

Baptista

 I know him well; you are welcome for his sake.   70

Gremio

 Saving your tale, Petruchio, I pray,

 Let us that are poor petitioners speak too.

 Bacare! you are marvellous forward.

Petruchio

 O, pardon me, Signior Gremio! I would fain be doing.

Gremio

 I doubt it not, sir; but you will curse your wooing. 75

 Neighbour, this is a gift very grateful, I am sure of it. To

 express the like kindness, myself, that have been more

 kindly beholding to you than any, freely give unto you

 this young scholar *[presenting* LUCENTIO*]* that hath been

 long studying at Rheims; as cunning in Greek, Latin, and 80

 other languages, as the other in music and mathematics.

 His name is Cambio. Pray accept his service.

Baptista

 A thousand thanks, Signior Gremio. Welcome, good

 Cambio. *[To* TRANIO*]* But, gentle sir, methinks you walk

 like a stranger. May I be so bold to know the cause of 85

 your coming?

Tranio

 Pardon me, sir, the boldness is mine own

 That, being a stranger in this city here,

 Do make myself a suitor to your daughter,

 Unto Bianca, fair and virtuous.   90

 Nor is your firm resolve unknown to me

 In the preferment of the eldest sister.

 This liberty is all that I request –

 That, upon knowledge of my parentage,

95   I may have welcome 'mongst the rest that woo,
And free access and favour as the rest.
And toward the education of your daughters
I here bestow a simple instrument,
And this small packet of Greek and Latin books.
100   If you accept them, then their worth is great.

Baptista
Lucentio is your name? Of whence, I pray?

Tranio
Of Pisa, sir; son to Vincentio.

Baptista
A mighty man of Pisa. By report
I know him well. You are very welcome, sir.
105   Take you the lute, and you the set of books;
You shall go see your pupils presently.
Holla, within!

[Enter a Servant.]

            Sirrah, lead these gentlemen
To my daughters; and tell them both
These are their tutors. Bid them use them well.

[Exit Servant leading HORTENSIO *carrying the lute and*
LUCENTIO *with the books.]*

110   We will go walk a little in the orchard,
And then to dinner. You are passing welcome,
And so I pray you all to think yourselves.

Petruchio
Signior Baptista, my business asketh haste,
And every day I cannot come to woo.
115   You knew my father well, and in him me,
Left solely heir to all his lands and goods,
Which I have bettered rather than decreas'd.
Then tell me, if I get your daughter's love,
What dowry shall I have with her to wife?

Baptista

    After my death, the one half of my lands   120

    And, in possession, twenty thousand crowns.

Petruchio

    And for that dowry, I'll assure her of

    Her widowhood, be it that she survive me,

    In all my lands and leases whatsoever.

    Let specialties be therefore drawn between us,   125

    That covenants may be kept on either hand.

Baptista

    Ay, when the special thing is well obtain'd,

    That is, her love; for that is all in all.

Petruchio

    Why, that is nothing; for I tell you, father,

    I am as peremptory as she proud-minded;   130

    And where two raging fires meet together,

    They do consume the thing that feeds their fury.

    Though little fire grows great with little wind,

    Yet extreme gusts will blow out fire and all.

    So I to her, and so she yields to me;   135

    For I am rough, and woo not like a babe.

Baptista

    Well mayst thou woo, and happy be thy speed!

    But be thou arm'd for some unhappy words.

Petruchio

    Ay, to the proof, as mountains are for winds,

    That shake not though they blow perpetually.   140

    [Re-enter HORTENSIO, *with his head broke.]*

Baptista

    How now, my friend! Why dost thou look so pale?

Hortensio

    For fear, I promise you, if I look pale.

Baptista

    What, will my daughter prove a good musician?

Hortensio

    I think she'll sooner prove a soldier:

145   Iron may hold with her, but never lutes.
    Baptista
        Why, then thou canst not break her to the lute?
    Hortensio
        Why, no; for she hath broke the lute to me.
        I did but tell her she mistook her frets,
        And bow'd her hand to teach her fingering,
150   When, with a most impatient devilish spirit,
        'Frets, call you these?' quoth she 'I'll fume with them'.
        And with that word she struck me on the head,
        And through the instrument my pate made way;
        And there I stood amazed for a while,
155   As on a pillory, looking through the lute,
        While she did call me rascal fiddler
        And twangling Jack, with twenty such vile terms,
        As had she studied to misuse me so.
    Petruchio
        Now, by the world, it is a lusty wench;
160   I love her ten times more than e'er I did.
        O, how I long to have some chat with her!
    Baptista
        Well, go with me, and be not so discomfited;
        Proceed in practice with my younger daughter;
        She's apt to learn, and thankful for good turns.
165   Signior Petruchio, will you go with us,
        Or shall I send my daughter Kate to you?
    Petruchio
        I pray you do.

                    [Exeunt all but PETRUCHIO.*]*

                    I'll attend her here,
        And woo her with some spirit when she comes.
        Say that she rail; why, then I'll tell her plain
170   She sings as sweetly as a nightingale.
        Say that she frown; I'll say she looks as clear
        As morning roses newly wash'd with dew.
        Say she be mute, and will not speak a word;

Then I'll commend her volubility,
And say she uttereth piercing eloquence. 175
If she do bid me pack, I'll give her thanks,
As though she bid me stay by her a week;
If she deny to wed, I'll crave the day
When I shall ask the banns, and when be married.
But here she comes; and now, Petruchio, speak. 180

[Enter KATHERINA.*]*

Good morrow, Kate – for that's your name, I hear.
Katherina
　Well have you heard, but something hard of hearing:
　They call me Katherine that do talk of me.
Petruchio
　You lie, in faith, for you are call'd plain Kate,
　And bonny Kate, and sometimes Kate the curst; 185
　But, Kate, the prettiest Kate in Christendom,
　Kate of Kate Hall, my super-dainty Kate,
　For dainties are all Kates, and therefore, Kate,
　Take this of me, Kate of my consolation –
　Hearing thy mildness prais'd in every town, 190
　Thy virtues spoke of, and thy beauty sounded,
　Yet not so deeply as to thee belongs,
　Myself am mov'd to woo thee for my wife.
Katherina
　Mov'd! in good time! Let him that mov'd you hither
　Remove you hence. I knew you at the first 195
　You were a moveable.
Petruchio
　　　　　　Why, what's a moveable?
Katherina
　A join'd-stool.
Petruchio
　　　　　Thou hast hit it. Come, sit on me.
Katherina
　Asses are made to bear, and so are you.

Petruchio
Women are made to bear, and so are you.
Katherina
200 No such jade as you, if me you mean.
Petruchio
Alas, good Kate, I will not burden thee!
For, knowing thee to be but young and light –
Katherina
Too light for such a swain as you to catch;
And yet as heavy as my weight should be.
Petruchio
Should be! should – buzz!
Katherina
205   Well ta'en, and like a buzzard.
Petruchio
O, slow-wing'd turtle, shall a buzzard take thee?
Katherina
Ay, for a turtle, as he takes a buzzard.
Petruchio
Come, come, you wasp; i' faith, you are too angry.
Katherina
If I be waspish, best beware my sting.
Petruchio
210 My remedy is then to pluck it out.
Katherina
Ay, if the fool could find it where it lies.
Petruchio
Who knows not where a wasp does wear his sting?
In his tail.
Katherina
In his tongue.
Petruchio
215 Whose tongue?
Katherina
Yours, if you talk of tales; and so farewell.
Petruchio
What, with my tongue in your tail? Nay, come again,
Good Kate; I am a gentleman.

Katherina

That I'll try.

[She strikes him.]

Petruchio
I swear I'll cuff you, if you strike again.
Katherina
So may you lose your arms.   220
If you strike me, you are no gentleman;
And if no gentleman, why then no arms.
Petruchio
A herald, Kate? O, put me in thy books!
Katherina
What is your crest – a coxcomb?
Petruchio
A combless cock, so Kate will be my hen.   225
Katherina
No cock of mine: you crow too like a craven.
Petruchio
Nay, come, Kate, come; you must not look so sour.
Katherina
It is my fashion, when I see a crab.
Petruchio
Why, here's no crab; and therefore look not sour.
Katherina
There is, there is.   230
Petruchio
Then show it me.
Katherina

Had I a glass I would.

Petruchio
What, you mean my face?
Katherina

Well aim'd of such a young one.

Petruchio
Now, by Saint George, I am too young for you.
Katherina
Yet you are wither'd.

Petruchio

           'Tis with cares.

Katherina

              I care not.

Petruchio

235   Nay, hear you, Kate – in sooth, you scape not so.

Katherina

    I chafe you, if I tarry; let me go.

Petruchio

    No, not a whit; I find you passing gentle.
    'Twas told me you were rough, and coy, and sullen,
    And now I find report a very liar;
240   For thou art pleasant, gamesome, passing courteous,
    But slow in speech, yet sweet as springtime flowers.
    Thou canst not frown, thou canst not look askance,
    Nor bite the lip, as angry wenches will,
    Nor hast thou pleasure to be cross in talk;
245   But thou with mildness entertain'st thy wooers;
    With gentle conference, soft and affable.
    Why does the world report that Kate doth limp?
    O sland'rous world! Kate like the hazel-twig
    Is straight and slender, and as brown in hue
250   As hazel-nuts, and sweeter than the kernels.
    O, let me see thee walk. Thou dost not halt.

Katherina

    Go, fool, and whom thou keep'st command.

Petruchio

    Did ever Dian so become a grove
    As Kate this chamber with her princely gait?
255   O, be thou Dian, and let her be Kate;
    And then let Kate be chaste, and Dian sportful!

Katherina

    Where did you study all this goodly speech?

Petruchio

    It is extempore, from my mother wit.

Katherina

    A witty mother! witless else her son.

Petruchio
 Am I not wise?   260
Katherina
 Yes, keep you warm.
Petruchio
 Marry, so I mean, sweet Katherine, in thy bed.
 And therefore, setting all this chat aside,
 Thus in plain terms: your father hath consented
 That you shall be my wife; your dowry 'greed on;   265
 And will you, nill you, I will marry you.
 Now, Kate, I am a husband for your turn;
 For, by this light, whereby I see thy beauty,
 Thy beauty that doth make me like thee well,
 Thou must be married to no man but me;   270
 For I am he am born to tame you, Kate,
 And bring you from a wild Kate to a Kate
 Conformable as other household Kates.

   [Re-enter BAPTISTA, GREMIO, and TRANIO.]

 Here comes your father. Never make denial;
 I must and will have Katherine to my wife.   275
Baptista
 Now, Signior Petruchio, how speed you with my
  daughter?
Petruchio
 How but well, sir? how but well?
 It were impossible I should speed amiss.
Baptista
 Why, how now, daughter Katherine, in your dumps?
Katherina
 Call you me daughter? Now I promise you   280
 You have show'd a tender fatherly regard
 To wish me wed to one half lunatic,
 A mad-cap ruffian and a swearing Jack,
 That thinks with oaths to face the matter out.
Petruchio
 Father, 'tis thus: yourself and all the world   285

That talk'd of her have talk'd amiss of her.
If she be curst, it is for policy,
For she's not froward, but modest as the dove;
She is not hot, but temperate as the morn;
290   For patience she will prove a second Grissel,
And Roman Lucrece for her chastity.
And, to conclude, we have 'greed so well together
That upon Sunday is the wedding-day.

Katherina
I'll see thee hang'd on Sunday first.

Gremio
295   Hark, Petruchio; she says she'll see thee hang'd first.

Tranio
Is this your speeding? Nay, then good-night our part!

Petruchio
Be patient, gentlemen. I choose her for myself;
If she and I be pleas'd, what's that to you?
'Tis bargain'd 'twixt us twain, being alone,
300   That she shall still be curst in company.
I tell you 'tis incredible to believe
How much she loves me – O, the kindest Kate!
She hung about my neck, and kiss on kiss
She vied so fast, protesting oath on oath,
305   That in a twink she won me to her love.
O, you are novices! 'Tis a world to see
How tame, when men and women are alone,
A meacock wretch can make the curstest shrew.
Give me thy hand, Kate; I will unto Venice,
310   To buy apparel 'gainst the wedding-day.
Provide the feast, father, and bid the guests;
I will be sure my Katherine shall be fine.

Baptista
I know not what to say; but give me your hands.
God send you joy, Petruchio! 'Tis a match.

Gremio, Tranio
315   Amen, say we; we will be witnesses.

Petruchio
Father, and wife, and gentlemen, adieu.
I will to Venice; Sunday comes apace;
We will have rings and things, and fine array;
And kiss me, Kate; we will be married a Sunday.

[*Exeunt* PETRUCHIO *and* KATHERINA *severally.*]

Gremio
Was ever match clapp'd up so suddenly? 320
Baptista
Faith, gentlemen, now I play a merchant's part,
And venture madly on a desperate mart.
Tranio
'Twas a commodity lay fretting by you;
'Twill bring you gain, or perish on the seas.
Baptista
The gain I seek is quiet in the match. 325
Gremio
No doubt but he hath got a quiet catch.
But now, Baptista, to your younger daughter:
Now is the day we long have looked for;
I am your neighbour, and was suitor first.
Tranio
And I am one that love Bianca more 330
Than words can witness or your thoughts can guess.
Gremio
Youngling, thou canst not love so dear as I.
Tranio
Greybeard, thy love doth freeze.
Gremio
                                        But thine doth fry.
Skipper, stand back; 'tis age that nourisheth.
Tranio
But youth in ladies' eyes that flourisheth. 335
Baptista
Content you, gentlemen; I will compound this strife.
'Tis deeds must win the prize, and he of both

53

That can assure my daughter greatest dower
Shall have my Bianca's love.
340   Say, Signior Gremio, what can you assure her?

Gremio
   First, as you know, my house within the city
   Is richly furnished with plate and gold,
   Basins and ewers to lave her dainty hands;
   My hangings all of Tyrian tapestry;
345   In ivory coffers I have stuff'd my crowns;
   In cypress chests my arras counterpoints,
   Costly apparel, tents, and canopies,
   Fine linen, Turkey cushions boss'd with pearl,
   Valance of Venice gold in needle-work;
350   Pewter and brass, and all things that belongs
   To house or housekeeping. Then at my farm
   I have a hundred milch-kine to the pail,
   Six score fat oxen standing in my stalls,
   And all things answerable to this portion.
355   Myself am struck in years, I must confess;
   And if I die to-morrow this is hers,
   If whilst I live she will be only mine.

Tranio
   That 'only' came well in. Sir, list to me:
   I am my father's heir and only son;
360   If I may have your daughter to my wife,
   I'll leave her houses three or four as good
   Within rich Pisa's walls as any one
   Old Signior Gremio has in Padua;
   Besides two thousand ducats by the year
365   Of fruitful land, all which shall be her jointure.
   What, have I pinch'd you, Signior Gremio?

Gremio
   Two thousand ducats by the year of land!
   [Aside] My land amounts not to so much in all. –
   That she shall have, besides an argosy
370   That now is lying in Marseilles road.
   What, have I chok'd you with an argosy?

Tranio
  Gremio, 'tis known my father hath no less
  Than three great argosies, besides two galliasses,
  And twelve tight galleys. These I will assure her,
  And twice as much whate'er thou off'rest next.   375
Gremio
  Nay, I have off'red all; I have no more;
  And she can have no more than all I have;
  If you like me, she shall have me and mine.
Tranio
  Why, then the maid is mine from all the world
  By your firm promise; Gremio is out-vied.   380
Baptista
  I must confess your offer is the best;
  And let your father make her the assurance,
  She is your own. Else, you must pardon me;
  If you should die before him, where's her dower?
Tranio
  That's but a cavil; he is old, I young.   385
Gremio
  And may not young men die as well as old?
Baptista
  Well, gentlemen,
  I am thus resolv'd: on Sunday next you know
  My daughter Katherine is to be married;
  Now, on the Sunday following shall Bianca   390
  Be bride to you, if you make this assurance;
  If not, to Signior Gremio.
  And so I take my leave, and thank you both.
Gremio
  Adieu, good neighbour.

[Exit BAPTISTA.*]*

                    Now, I fear thee not.
  Sirrah young gamester, your father were a fool   395
  To give thee all, and in his waning age
  Set foot under thy table. Tut, a toy!

An old Italian fox is not so kind, my boy.

[Exit.]

Tranio

A vengeance on your crafty withered hide!
400 Yet I have fac'd it with a card of ten.
'Tis in my head to do my master good:
I see no reason but suppos'd Lucentio
Must get a father, call'd suppos'd Vincentio;
And that's a wonder – fathers commonly
405 Do get their children; but in this case of wooing
A child shall get a sire, if I fail not of my cunning.

[Exit.]

ACT THREE
Scene I

Padua. Baptista's house.

[Enter LUCENTIO *as Cambio,* HORTENSIO *as Licio, and*
BIANCA.*]*

Lucentio
  Fiddler, forbear; you grow too forward, sir.
  Have you so soon forgot the entertainment
  Her sister Katherine welcom'd you withal?
Hortensio
  But, wrangling pedant, this is
  The patroness of heavenly harmony.   5
  Then give me leave to have prerogative;
  And when in music we have spent an hour,
  Your lecture shall have leisure for as much.
Lucentio
  Preposterous ass, that never read so far
  To know the cause why music was ordain'd!   10
  Was it not to refresh the mind of man
  After his studies or his usual pain?
  Then give me leave to read philosophy,
  And while I pause serve in your harmony.
Hortensio
  Sirrah, I will not bear these braves of thine.   15
Bianca
  Why, gentlemen, you do me double wrong
  To strive for that which resteth in my choice.
  I am no breeching scholar in the schools,
  I'll not be tied to hours nor 'pointed times,
  But learn my lessons as I please myself.   20
  And to cut off all strife: here sit we down;
  Take you your instrument, play you the whiles;
  His lecture will be done ere you have tun'd.

Hortensio
You'll leave his lecture when I am in tune?
Lucentio
25 That will be never – tune your instrument.
Bianca
Where left we last?
Lucentio
Here, madam:
'Hic ibat Simois, hic est Sigeia tellus,
Hic steterat Priami regia celsa senis'.
Bianca
30 Construe them.
Lucentio
'Hic ibat' as I told you before – 'Simois' I am Lucentio
– 'his est' son unto Vincentio of Pisa – 'Sigeia tellus'
disguised thus to get your love – 'Hic steterat' and that
Lucentio that comes a-wooing – 'Priami' is my man
35 Tranio – 'regia' bearing my port – 'celsa senis' that we
might beguile the old pantaloon.
Hortensio
Madam, my instrument's in tune.
Bianca
Let's hear. O fie! the treble jars.
Lucentio
Spit in the hole, man, and tune again.
Bianca
40 Now let me see if I can construe it: 'Hic ibat Simois' I
know you not – 'hic est Sigeia tellu' I trust you not –
'Hic steterat Priami' take heed he hear us not – 'regia'
presume not – 'celsa senis' despair not.
Hortensio
Madam. 'tis now in tune.
Lucentio
                    All but the bass.
Hortensio
45 The bass is right; 'tis the base knave that jars.
[Aside] How fiery and forward our pedant is!

Now, for my life, the knave doth court my love.
Pedascule, I'll watch you better yet.

Bianca

In time I may believe, yet I mistrust.

Lucentio

Mistrust it not – for, sure, AEacides   50
Was Ajax, call'd so from his grandfather.

Bianca

I must believe my master; else, I promise you,
I should be arguing still upon that doubt;
But let it rest. Now, Licio, to you.
Good master, take it not unkindly, pray,   55
That I have been thus pleasant with you both.

Hortensio

[To LUCENTIO] You may go walk and give me leave
    awhile;
My lessons make no music in three parts.

Lucentio

Are you so formal, sir? Well, I must wait,
[Aside] And watch withal; for, but I be deceiv'd,   60
Our fine musician groweth amorous.

Hortensio

Madam, before you touch the instrument
To learn the order of my fingering,
I must begin with rudiments of art,
To teach you gamut in a briefer sort,   65
More pleasant, pithy, and effectual,
Than hath been taught by any of my trade;
And there it is in writing fairly drawn.

Bianca

Why, I am past my gamut long ago.

Hortensio

Yet read the gamut of Hortensio.   70

Bianca

[Reads]
'"Gamut" I am, the ground of all accord –
'A re' to plead Hortensio's passion –

'B mi' Bianca, take him for thy lord –
'C fa ut' that loves with all affection –
75   'D sol re' one clef, two notes have I –
'E la mi' show pity or I die.'
Call you this gamut? Tut, I like it not!
Old fashions please me best; I am not so nice
To change true rules for odd inventions.

[Enter a Servant.]

Servant
80   Mistress, your father prays you leave your books
And help to dress your sister's chamber up.
You know to-morrow is the wedding-day.
Bianca
Farewell, sweet masters, both; I must be gone.

[Exeunt BIANCA and Servant.]

Lucentio
Faith, mistress, then I have no cause to stay.   *[Exit.]*
Hortensio
85   But I have cause to pry into this pedant;
Methinks he looks as though he were in love.
Yet if thy thoughts, Bianca, be so humble
To cast thy wand'ring eyes on every stale –
Seize thee that list. If once I find thee ranging,
90   Hortensio will be quit with thee by changing.

[Exit.]

Scene II

Padua. Before Baptista's house.

[Enter BAPTISTA, GREMIO, TRANIO *as Lucentio,*
KATHERINA, BIANCA, LUCENTIO *as Cambio, and*
Attendants.]

Baptista
  [To TRANIO*]* Signior Lucentio, this is the 'pointed day
  That Katherine and Petruchio should be married,
  And yet we hear not of our son-in-law.
  What will be said? What mockery will it be
  To want the bridegroom when the priest attends   5
  To speak the ceremonial rites of marriage!
  What says Lucentio to this shame of ours?
Katherina
  No shame but mine; I must, forsooth, be forc'd
  To give my hand, oppos'd against my heart,
  Unto a mad-brain rudesby, full of spleen,   10
  Who woo'd in haste and means to wed at leisure.
  I told you, I, he was a frantic fool,
  Hiding his bitter jests in blunt behaviour;
  And, to be noted for a merry man,
  He'll woo a thousand, 'point the day of marriage,   15
  Make friends invited, and proclaim the banns;
  Yet never means to wed where he hath woo'd.
  Now must the world point at poor Katherine,
  And say 'Lo, there is mad Petruchio's wife,
  If it would please him come and marry her!'   20
Tranio
  Patience, good Katherine, and Baptista too.
  Upon my life, Petruchio means but well,
  Whatever fortune stays him from his word.
  Though he be blunt, I know him passing wise;
  Though he be merry, yet withal he's honest.   25
Katherina
  Would Katherine had never seen him though!

[Exit, weeping, followed by BIANCA *and others.]*

Baptista

Go, girl, I cannot blame thee now to weep,
For such an injury would vex a very saint;
Much more a shrew of thy impatient humour.

[Enter BIONDELLO*.]*

Biondello

30 Master, master! News, and such old news as you never
heard of!

Baptista

Is it new and old too? How may that be?

Biondello

Why, is it not news to hear of Petruchio's coming?

Baptista

Is he come?

Biondello

35 Why, no, sir.

Baptista

What then?

Biondello

He is coming.

Baptista

When will he be here?

Biondello

When he stands where I am and sees you there.

Tranio

40 But, say, what to thine old news?

Bianca

Why, Petruchio is coming – in a new hat and an old
jerkin; a pair of old breeches thrice turn'd; a pair of boots
that have been candle-cases, one buckled, another lac'd;
an old rusty sword ta'en out of the town armoury, with
45 a broken hilt, and chapeless; with two broken points;
his horse hipp'd, with an old mothy saddle and stirrups
of no kindred; besides, possess'd with the glanders and
like to mose in the chine, troubled with the lampass,

infected with the fashions, full of windgalls, sped
with spavins, rayed with the yellows, past cure of the   50
fives, stark spoil'd with the staggers, begnawn with the
bots, sway'd in the back and shoulder-shotten, near-
legg'd before, and with a half-cheek'd bit, and a head-
stall of sheep's leather which, being restrain'd to keep
him from stumbling, hath been often burst, and now   55
repaired with knots; one girth six times piec'd, and a
woman's crupper of velure, which hath two letters for
her name fairly set down in studs, and here and there
piec'd with pack-thread.

Baptista

Who comes with him?   60

Biondello

O, sir, his lackey, for all the world caparison'd like the
horse – with a linen stock on one leg and a kersey boot-
hose on the other, gart'red with a red and blue list; an
old hat, and the humour of forty fancies prick'd in't for
a feather; a monster, a very monster in apparel, and not   65
like a Christian footboy or a gentleman's lackey.

Tranio

'Tis some odd humour pricks him to this fashion;
Yet oftentimes he goes but mean-apparell'd.

Baptista

I am glad he's come, howsoe'er he comes.

Biondello

Why, sir, he comes not.   70

Baptista

Didst thou not say he comes?

Biondello

Who? that Petruchio came?

Baptista

Ay, that Petruchio came.

Biondello

No, sir; I say his horse comes with him on his back.

Baptista

Why, that's all one.   75

Biondello

           Nay, by Saint Jamy,
           I hold you a penny,
           A horse and a man
           Is more than one,
80   And yet not many.

      [Enter PETRUCHIO and GRUMIO.]

Petruchio
    Come, where be these gallants?
    Who's at home?
Baptista
    You are welcome, sir.
Petruchio
                And yet I come not well.
Baptista
    And yet you halt not.
Tranio
              Not so well apparell'd
85 As I wish you were.
Petruchio
    Were it better, I should rush in thus.
    But where is Kate? Where is my lovely bride?
    How does my father? Gentles, methinks you frown;
    And wherefore gaze this goodly company
90 As if they saw some wondrous monument,
    Some comet or unusual prodigy?
Baptista
    Why, sir, you know this is your wedding-day.
    First were we sad, fearing you would not come;
    Now sadder, that you come so unprovided.
95 Fie, doff this habit, shame to your estate,
    An eye-sore to our solemn festival!
Tranio
    And tell us what occasion of import
    Hath all so long detain'd you from your wife,
    And sent you hither so unlike yourself?

Petruchio

    Tedious it were to tell, and harsh to hear;   100
    Sufficeth I am come to keep my word,
    Though in some part enforced to digress,
    Which at more leisure I will so excuse
    As you shall well be satisfied withal.
    But where is Kate? I stay too long from her;   105
    The morning wears, 'tis time we were at church.

Tranio

    See not your bride in these unreverent robes;
    Go to my chamber, put on clothes of mine.

Petruchio

    Not I, believe me; thus I'll visit her.

Baptista

    But thus, I trust, you will not marry her.   110

Petruchio

    Good sooth, even thus; therefore ha' done with words;
    To me she's married, not unto my clothes.
    Could I repair what she will wear in me
    As I can change these poor accoutrements,
    'Twere well for Kate and better for myself.   115
    But what a fool am I to chat with you,
    When I should bid good morrow to my bride
    And seal the title with a lovely kiss!

[Exeunt PETRUCHIO *and* GRUMIO.*]*

Tranio

    He hath some meaning in his mad attire.
    We will persuade him, be it possible,   120
    To put on better ere he go to church.

Baptista

    I'll after him and see the event of this.

[Exeunt BAPTISTA, GREMIO, BIONDELLO, *and*
Attendants.*]*

Tranio

    But to her love concerneth us to add

Her father's liking; which to bring to pass,
125 As I before imparted to your worship,
I am to get a man – whate'er he be
It skills not much; we'll fit him to our turn –
And he shall be Vincentio of Pisa,
And make assurance here in Padua
130 Of greater sums than I have promised.
So shall you quietly enjoy your hope
And marry sweet Bianca with consent.

Lucentio

Were it not that my fellow school-master
Doth watch Bianca's steps so narrowly,
135 'Twere good, methinks, to steal our marriage;
Which once perform'd, let all the world say no,
I'll keep mine own despite of all the world.

Tranio

That by degrees we mean to look into
And watch our vantage in this business;
140 We'll over-reach the greybeard, Gremio,
The narrow-prying father, Minola,
The quaint musician, amorous Licio –
All for my master's sake, Lucentio.

[Re-enter GREMIO.]

Signior Gremio, came you from the church?

Gremio

145 As willingly as e'er I came from school.

Tranio

And is the bride and bridegroom coming home?

Gremio

A bridegroom, say you? 'Tis a groom indeed,
A grumbling groom, and that the girl shall find.

Tranio

Curster than she? Why, 'tis impossible.

Gremio

150 Why, he's a devil, a devil, a very fiend.

Tranio
    Why, she's a devil, a devil, the devil's dam.
Gremio
    Tut, she's a lamb, a dove, a fool, to him!
    I'll tell you, Sir Lucentio: when the priest
    Should ask if Katherine should be his wife,
    'Ay, by gogs-wouns' quoth he, and swore so loud   155
    That, all amaz'd, the priest let fall the book;
    And as he stoop'd again to take it up,
    This mad-brain'd bridegroom took him such a cuff
    That down fell priest and book, and book and priest.
    'Now take them up,' quoth he 'if any list.'   160
Tranio
    What said the wench, when he rose again?
Gremio
    Trembled and shook, for why he stamp'd and swore
    As if the vicar meant to cozen him.
    But after many ceremonies done
    He calls for wine: 'A health!' quoth he, as if   165
    He had been abroad, carousing to his mates
    After a storm; quaff'd off the muscadel,
    And threw the sops all in the sexton's face,
    Having no other reason
    But that his beard grew thin and hungerly   170
    And seem'd to ask him sops as he was drinking.
    This done, he took the bride about the neck,
    And kiss'd her lips with such a clamorous smack
    That at the parting all the church did echo.
    And I, seeing this, came thence for very shame;   175
    And after me, I know, the rout is coming.
    Such a mad marriage never was before.
    Hark, hark! I hear the minstrels play.

[Music plays.]

[Enter PETRUCHIO, KATHERINA, BIANCA, BAPTISTA,
HORTENSIO, GRUMIO, *and Train.]*

Petruchio
    Gentlemen and friends, I thank you for your pains.
180   I know you think to dine with me to-day,
    And have prepar'd great store of wedding cheer;
    But so it is – my haste doth call me hence,
    And therefore here I mean to take my leave.

Baptista
    Is't possible you will away tonight?

Petruchio
185   I must away to-day before night come.
    Make it no wonder; if you knew my business,
    You would entreat me rather go than stay.
    And, honest company, I thank you all
    That have beheld me give away myself
190   To this most patient, sweet, and virtuous wife.
    Dine with my father, drink a health to me,
    For I must hence; and farewell to you all.

Tranio
    Let us entreat you stay till after dinner.

Petruchio
    It may not be.

Gremio
             Let me entreat you.

Petruchio
    It cannot be.

Katherina
195   Let me entreat you.

Petruchio
    I am content.

Katherina
            Are you content to stay?

Petruchio
    I am content you shall entreat me stay;
    But yet not stay, entreat me how you can.

Katherina
    Now, if you love me, stay.

Petruchio

       Grumio, my horse.

Grumio

 Ay, sir, they be ready; the oats have eaten the horses. 200

Katherina

 Nay, then,
 Do what thou canst, I will not go to-day;
 No, nor to-morrow, not till I please myself.
 The door is open, sir; there lies your way;
 You may be jogging whiles your boots are green;
 For me, I'll not be gone till I please myself. 205
 'Tis like you'll prove a jolly surly groom
 That take it on you at the first so roundly.

Petruchio

 O Kate, content thee; prithee be not angry.

Katherina

 I will be angry; what hast thou to do?
 Father, be quiet; he shall stay my leisure. 210

Gremio

 Ay, marry, sir, now it begins to work.

Katherina

 Gentlemen, forward to the bridal dinner.
 I see a woman may be made a fool
 If she had not a spirit to resist.

Petruchio

 They shall go forward, Kate, at thy command. 215
 Obey the bride, you that attend on her;
 Go to the feast, revel and domineer,
 Carouse full measure to her maidenhead;
 Be mad and merry, or go hang yourselves.
 But for my bonny Kate, she must with me. 220
 Nay, look not big, nor stamp, nor stare, nor fret;
 I will be master of what is mine own –
 She is my goods, my chattels, she is my house,
 My household stuff, my field, my barn,
 My horse, my ox, my ass, my any thing, 225
 And here she stands; touch her whoever dare;

I'll bring mine action on the proudest he
That stops my way in Padua. Grumio,
Draw forth thy weapon; we are beset with thieves;
230   Rescue thy mistress, if thou be a man.
Fear not, sweet wench; they shall not touch thee,
    Kate;
I'll buckler thee against a million.

[Exeunt PETRUCHIO, KATHERINA, *and* GRUMIO.]

Baptista
  Nay, let them go, a couple of quiet ones.
Gremio
  Went they not quickly, I should die with laughing.
Tranio
235   Of all mad matches, never was the like.
Lucentio
  Mistress, what's your opinion of your sister?
Bianca
  That, being mad herself, she's madly mated.
Gremio
  I warrant him, Petruchio is Kated.
Baptista
  Neighbours and friends, though bride and bridegroom
    wants
240   For to supply the places at the table,
You know there wants no junkets at the feast.
Lucentio, you shall supply the bridegroom's place;
And let Bianca take her sister's room.
Tranio
  Shall sweet Bianca practise how to bride it?
Baptista
245   She shall, Lucentio. Come, gentlemen, let's go.

[Exeunt.]

ACT FOUR
Scene I

Petruchio's country house.

[Enter GRUMIO.]

Grumio

Fie, fie on all tired jades, on all mad masters, and all
foul ways! Was ever man so beaten? Was ever man
so ray'd? Was ever man so weary? I am sent before to
make a fire, and they are coming after to warm them.
Now were not I a little pot and soon hot, my very lips   5
might freeze to my teeth, my tongue to the roof of my
mouth, my heart in my belly, ere I should come by a
fire to thaw me. But I with blowing the fire shall warm
myself; for, considering the weather, a taller man than
I will take cold. Holla, ho! Curtis!   10

[Enter CURTIS.]

Curtis

Who is that calls so coldly?

Grumio

A piece of ice. If thou doubt it, thou mayst slide from
my shoulder to my heel with no greater a run but my
head and my neck. A fire, good Curtis.

Curtis

Is my master and his wife coming, Grumio?   15

Grumio

O, ay, Curtis, ay; and therefore fire, fire; cast on no
water.

Curtis

Is she so hot a shrew as she's reported?

Grumio

She was, good Curtis, before this frost; but thou
know'st winter tames man, woman, and beast; for it   20

hath tam'd my old master, and my new mistress, and myself, fellow Curtis.

Curtis

Away, you three-inch fool! I am no beast.

Grumio

Am I but three inches? Why, thy horn is a foot, and so
25 long am I at the least. But wilt thou make a fire, or shall I complain on thee to our mistress, whose hand – she being now at hand – thou shalt soon feel, to thy cold comfort, for being slow in thy hot office?

Curtis

I prithee, good Grumio, tell me how goes the world?

Grumio

30 A cold world, Curtis, in every office but thine; and therefore fire. Do thy duty, and have thy duty, for my master and mistress are almost frozen to death.

Curtis

There's fire ready; and therefore, good Grumio, the news?

Grumio

35 Why, 'Jack boy! ho, boy!' and as much news as wilt thou.

Curtis

Come, you are so full of cony-catching!

Grumio

Why, therefore, fire; for I have caught extreme cold. Where's the cook? Is supper ready, the house trimm'd,
40 rushes strew'd, cobwebs swept, the serving-men in their new fustian, their white stockings, and every officer his wedding-garment on? Be the jacks fair within, the jills fair without, the carpets laid, and everything in order?

Curtis

All ready; and therefore, I pray thee, news.

Grumio

45 First know my horse is tired; my master and mistress fall'n out.

Curtis

How?

Grumio

Out of their saddles into the dirt; and thereby hangs
a tale.

Curtis

Let's ha't, good Grumio.   50

Grumio

Lend thine ear.

Curtis

Here.

Grumio

There.

[Striking him.]

Curtis

This 'tis to feel a tale, not to hear a tale.

Grumio

And therefore 'tis call'd a sensible tale; and this cuff was   55
but to knock at your ear and beseech list'ning. Now I
begin: Imprimis, we came down a foul hill, my master
riding behind my mistress –

Curtis

Both of one horse?

Grumio

What's that to thee?   60

Curtis

Why, a horse.

Grumio

Tell thou the tale. But hadst thou not cross'd me, thou
shouldst have heard how her horse fell and she under
her horse; thou shouldst have heard in how miry a
place, how she was bemoil'd, how he left her with the   65
horse upon her, how he beat me because her horse
stumbled, how she waded through the dirt to pluck
him off me, how he swore, how she pray'd that never
pray'd before, how I cried, how the horses ran away,

70 how her bridle was burst, how I lost my crupper – with
many things of worthy memory, which now shall die in
oblivion, and thou return unexperienc'd to thy grave.

Curtis
By this reck'ning he is more shrew than she.

Grumio
Ay, and that thou and the proudest of you all shall find
75 when he comes home. But what talk I of this? Call forth
Nathaniel, Joseph, Nicholas, Philip, Walter, Sugarsop,
and the rest; let their heads be sleekly comb'd, their
blue coats brush'd and their garters of an indifferent
knit; let them curtsy with their left legs, and not
80 presume to touch a hair of my master's horse-tail till
they kiss their hands. Are they all ready?

Curtis
They are.

Grumio
Call them forth.

Curtis
Do you hear, ho? You must meet my master, to
85 countenance my mistress.

Grumio
Why, she hath a face of her own.

Curtis
Who knows not that?

Grumio
Thou, it seems, that calls for company to countenance
her.

Curtis
90 I call them forth to credit her.

Grumio
Why, she comes to borrow nothing of them.

[Enter four or five Servants.]

Nathaniel
Welcome home, Grumio!

Philip

How now, Grumio!

Joseph

What, Grumio!

Nicholas

Fellow Grumio!   95

Nathaniel

How now, old lad!

Grumio

Welcome, you! – how now, you! – what, you! – fellow,
you! – and thus much for greeting. Now, my spruce
companions, is all ready, and all things neat?

Nathaniel

All things is ready. How near is our master?   100

Grumio

E'en at hand, alighted by this; and therefore be not –
Cock's passion, silence! I hear my master.

[Enter PETRUCHIO *and* KATHERINA.*]*

Petruchio

Where be these knaves? What, no man at door
To hold my stirrup nor to take my horse!
Where is Nathaniel, Gregory, Philip?   105

All Servants

Here, here, sir; here, sir.

Petruchio

Here, sir! here, sir! here, sir! here, sir!
You logger-headed and unpolish'd grooms!
What, no attendance? no regard? no duty?
Where is the foolish knave I sent before?   110

Grumio

Here, sir; as foolish as I was before.

Petruchio

You peasant swain! you whoreson malt-horse drudge!
Did I not bid thee meet me in the park
And bring along these rascal knaves with thee?

Grumio

115 Nathaniel's coat, sir, was not fully made,
     And Gabriel's pumps were all unpink'd i' th' heel;
     There was no link to colour Peter's hat,
     And Walter's dagger was not come from sheathing;
     There were none fine but Adam, Ralph, and Gregory;
120 The rest were ragged, old, and beggarly;
     Yet, as they are, here are they come to meet you.

Petruchio

     Go, rascals, go and fetch my supper in.

[Exeunt some of the Servants.]

[Sings]   Where is the life that late I led?
              Where are those –

125 Sit down, Kate, and welcome. Soud, soud, soud, soud!

[Re-enter Servants with supper.]

     Why, when, I say? Nay, good sweet Kate, be merry.
     Off with my boots, you rogues! you villains, when?

[Sings]   It was the friar of orders grey,
              As he forth walked on his way –

130 Out, you rogue! you pluck my foot awry;
     Take that, and mend the plucking off the other.

                                        [Strikes him.]

     Be merry, Kate. Some water, here, what, ho!

[Enter One with water.]

     Where's my spaniel Troilus? Sirrah, get you hence,
     And bid my cousin Ferdinand come hither:

[Exit Servants.]

135 One, Kate, that you must kiss and be acquainted with.
     Where are my slippers? Shall I have some water?
     Come, Kate, and wash, and welcome heartily.
     You whoreson villain! will you let it fall?

[Strikes him.]

Katherina
Patience, I pray you; 'twas a fault unwilling.
Petruchio
A whoreson, beetle-headed, flapear'd knave!   140
Come, Kate, sit down; I know you have a stomach.
Will you give thanks, sweet Kate, or else shall I?
What's this? Mutton?
I Servant
            Ay.
Petruchio
                Who brought it?
Peter
                     I.
Petruchio
'Tis burnt; and so is all the meat.
What dogs are these? Where is the rascal cook?   145
How durst you villains bring it from the dresser
And serve it thus to me that love it not?
There, take it to you, trenchers, cups, and all;

[Throws the meat, etc., at them.]

You heedless joltheads and unmanner'd slaves!
What, do you grumble? I'll be with you straight.   150

[Exeunt Servants.]

Katherina
I pray you, husband, be not so disquiet;
The meat was well, if you were so contented.
Petruchio
I tell thee, Kate, 'twas burnt and dried away,
And I expressly am forbid to touch it;
For it engenders choler, planteth anger;   155
And better 'twere that both of us did fast,
Since, of ourselves, ourselves are choleric,
Than feed it with such over-roasted flesh.
Be patient; to-morrow 't shall be mended,

160 And for this night we'll fast for company.
Come, I will bring thee to thy bridal chamber.

[Exeunt.]

[Re-enter Servants severally.]

Nathaniel
Peter, didst ever see the like?
Peter
He kills her in her own humour

[Re-enter CURTIS]

Grumio
Where is he?
Curtis
In her chamber. Making a sermon of continency to
165 her,
And rails, and swears, and rates, that she, poor soul,
Knows not which way to stand, to look, to speak,
And sits as one new risen from a dream.
Away, away! for he is coming hither.

[Exeunt.]

[Re-enter PETRUCHIO.]

Petruchio
170 Thus have I politicly begun my reign,
And 'tis my hope to end successfully.
My falcon now is sharp and passing empty,
And till she stoop she must not be full-gorg'd,
For then she never looks upon her lure.
175 Another way I have to man my haggard,
To make her come, and know her keeper's call,
That is, to watch her, as we watch these kites
That bate and beat, and will not be obedient.
She eat no meat to-day, nor none shall eat;
180 Last night she slept not, nor to-night she shall not;
As with the meat, some undeserved fault

I'll find about the making of the bed;
And here I'll fling the pillow, there the bolster,
This way the coverlet, another way the sheets;
Ay, and amid this hurly I intend   185
That all is done in reverend care of her –
And, in conclusion, she shall watch all night;
And if she chance to nod I'll rail and brawl
And with the clamour keep her still awake.
This is a way to kill a wife with kindness,   190
And thus I'll curb her mad and headstrong humour.
He that knows better how to tame a shrew,
Now let him speak; 'tis charity to show.

[Exit.]

Scene II

Padua. Before Baptista's house.

[Enter TRANIO *as Lucentio, and* HORTENSIO *as Licio.]*

Tranio

Is't possible, friend Licio, that Mistress Bianca
Doth fancy any other but Lucentio?
I tell you, sir, she bears me fair in hand.

Hortensio

Sir, to satisfy you in what I have said,
5   Stand by and mark the manner of his teaching.

[They stand aside.]

[Enter BIANCA *and* LUCENTIO *as Cambio.]*

Lucentio

Now, mistress, profit you in what you read?

Bianca

What, master, read you? First resolve me that.

Lucentio

I read that I profess, 'The Art to Love'.

Bianca

And may you prove, sir, master of your art!

Lucentio

10   While you, sweet dear, prove mistress of my heart.

[They retire.]

Hortensio

Quick proceeders, marry! Now tell me, I pray,
You that durst swear that your Mistress Bianca
Lov'd none in the world so well as Lucentio.

Tranio

O despiteful love! unconstant womankind!
15   I tell thee, Licio, this is wonderful.

Hortensio

Mistake no more; I am not Licio,
Nor a musician as I seem to be;

But one that scorn to live in this disguise
For such a one as leaves a gentleman
And makes a god of such a cullion.   20
Know, sir, that I am call'd Hortensio.

Tranio

Signior Hortensio, I have often heard
Of your entire affection to Bianca;
And since mine eyes are witness of her lightness,
I will with you, if you be so contented,   25
Forswear Bianca and her love for ever.

Hortensio

See, how they kiss and court! Signior Lucentio,
Here is my hand, and here I firmly vow
Never to woo her more, but do forswear her,
As one unworthy all the former favours   30
That I have fondly flatter'd her withal.

Tranio

And here I take the like unfeigned oath,
Never to marry with her though she would entreat;
Fie on her! See how beastly she doth court him!

Hortensio

Would all the world but he had quite forsworn!   35
For me, that I may surely keep mine oath,
I will be married to a wealthy widow
Ere three days pass, which hath as long lov'd me
As I have lov'd this proud disdainful haggard.
And so farewell, Signior Lucentio.   40
Kindness in women, not their beauteous looks,
Shall win my love; and so I take my leave,
In resolution as I swore before.

[Exit.]

Tranio

Mistress Bianca, bless you with such grace
As 'longeth to a lover's blessed case!   45
Nay, I have ta'en you napping, gentle love,
And have forsworn you with Hortensio.

Bianca
Tranio, you jest; but have you both forsworn me?
Tranio
Mistress, we have.
Lucentio
                   Then we are rid of Licio.
Tranio
50   I' faith, he'll have a lusty widow now,
That shall be woo'd and wedded in a day.
Bianca
God give him joy!
Tranio
Ay, and he'll tame her.
Bianca
                  He says so, Tranio.
Tranio
Faith, he is gone unto the taming-school.
Bianca
55   The taming-school! What, is there such a place?
Tranio
Ay, mistress; and Petruchio is the master,
That teacheth tricks eleven and twenty long,
To tame a shrew and charm her chattering tongue.

[Enter BIONDELLO.*]*

Biondello
O master, master, I have watch'd so long
60   That I am dog-weary; but at last I spied
An ancient angel coming down the hill
Will serve the turn.
Tranio
               What is he, Biondello?
Biondello
Master, a mercatante or a pedant,
I know not what; but formal in apparel,
65   In gait and countenance surely like a father.
Lucentio
And what of him, Tranio?

Tranio
    If he be credulous and trust my tale,
    I'll make him glad to seem Vincentio,
    And give assurance to Baptista Minola
    As if he were the right Vincentio.   70
    Take in your love, and then let me alone.

                [Exeunt LUCENTIO *and* BIANCA.]

                    [Enter a Pedant.]

Pedant
    God save you, sir!
Tranio
                        And you, sir; you are welcome.
    Travel you far on, or are you at the farthest?
Pedant
    Sir, at the farthest for a week or two;
    But then up farther, and as far as Rome;   75
    And so to Tripoli, if God lend me life.
Tranio
    What countryman, I pray?
Pedant
                                Of Mantua.
Tranio
    Of Mantua, sir? Marry, God forbid,
    And come to Padua, careless of your life!
Pedant
    My life, sir! How, I pray? For that goes hard.   80
Tranio
    'Tis death for any one in Mantua
    To come to Padua. Know you not the cause?
    Your ships are stay'd at Venice; and the Duke,
    For private quarrel 'twixt your Duke and him,
    Hath publish'd and proclaim'd it openly.   85
    'Tis marvel – but that you are but newly come,
    You might have heard it else proclaim'd about.
Pedant
    Alas, sir, it is worse for me than so!

For I have bills for money by exchange
90   From Florence, and must here deliver them.

Tranio

Well, sir, to do you courtesy,
This will I do, and this I will advise you –
First, tell me, have you ever been at Pisa?

Pedant

Ay, sir, in Pisa have I often been,
95   Pisa renowned for grave citizens.

Tranio

Among them know you one Vincentio?

Pedant

I know him not, but I have heard of him,
A merchant of incomparable wealth.

Tranio

He is my father, sir; and, sooth to say,
100   In count'nance somewhat doth resemble you.

Biondello

[*Aside*] As much as an apple doth an oyster, and all
    one.

Tranio

To save your life in this extremity,
This favour will I do you for his sake;
And think it not the worst of all your fortunes
105   That you are like to Sir Vincentio.
His name and credit shall you undertake,
And in my house you shall be friendly lodg'd;
Look that you take upon you as you should.
You understand me, sir. So shall you stay
110   Till you have done your business in the city.
If this be court'sy, sir, accept of it.

Pedant

O, sir, I do; and will repute you ever
The patron of my life and liberty.

Tranio

Then go with me to make the matter good.
115   This, by the way, I let you understand:

My father is here look'd for every day
To pass assurance of a dow'r in marriage
'Twixt me and one Baptista's daughter here.
In all these circumstances I'll instruct you.
Go with me to clothe you as becomes you.

[Exeunt.]

Scene III

Petruchio's house.

[Enter KATHERINA *and* GRUMIO.*]*

Grumio
No, no, forsooth; I dare not for my life.
Katherina
The more my wrong, the more his spite appears.
What, did he marry me to famish me?
Beggars that come unto my father's door
5   Upon entreaty have a present alms;
If not, elsewhere they meet with charity;
But I, who never knew how to entreat,
Nor never needed that I should entreat,
Am starv'd for meat, giddy for lack of sleep;
10   With oaths kept waking, and with brawling fed;
And that which spites me more than all these wants –
He does it under name of perfect love;
As who should say, if I should sleep or eat,
'Twere deadly sickness or else present death.
15   I prithee go and get me some repast;
I care not what, so it be wholesome food.
Grumio
What say you to a neat's foot?
Katherina
'Tis passing good; I prithee let me have it.
Grumio
I fear it is too choleric a meat.
20   How say you to a fat tripe finely broil'd?
Katherina
I like it well; good Grumio, fetch it me.
Grumio
I cannot tell; I fear 'tis choleric.
What say you to a piece of beef and mustard?
Katherina
A dish that I do love to feed upon.

Grumio
    Ay, but the mustard is too hot a little.   25
Katherina
    Why then the beef, and let the mustard rest.
Grumio
    Nay, then I will not; you shall have the mustard,
    Or else you get no beef of Grumio.
Katherina
    Then both, or one, or anything thou wilt.
Grumio
    Why then the mustard without the beef.   30
Katherina
    Go, get thee gone, thou false deluding slave,
                      [Beats him.]
    That feed'st me with the very name of meat.
    Sorrow on thee and all the pack of you
    That triumph thus upon my misery!
    Go, get thee gone, I say.   35

    [Enter PETRUCHIO, *and* HORTENSIO *with meat.]*

Petruchio
    How fares my Kate? What, sweeting, all amort?
Hortensio
    Mistress, what cheer?
Katherina
                 Faith, as cold as can be.
Petruchio
    Pluck up thy spirits, look cheerfully upon me.
    Here, love, thou seest how diligent I am,
    To dress thy meat myself, and bring it thee.   40
    I am sure, sweet Kate, this kindness merits thanks.
    What, not a word? Nay, then thou lov'st it not,
    And all my pains is sorted to no proof.
    Here, take away this dish.
Katherina
                 I pray you, let it stand.

Petruchio

45   The poorest service is repaid with thanks;
      And so shall mine, before you touch the meat.

Katherina

      I thank you, sir.

Hortensio

      Signior Petruchio, fie! you are to blame.
      Come, Mistress Kate, I'll bear you company.

Petruchio

50   *[Aside]* Eat it up all, Hortensio, if thou lovest me. –
      Much good do it unto thy gentle heart!
      Kate, eat apace. And now, my honey love,
      Will we return unto thy father's house
      And revel it as bravely as the best,

55   With silken coats and caps, and golden rings,
      With ruffs and cuffs and farthingales and things,
      With scarfs and fans and double change of brav'ry,
      With amber bracelets, beads, and all this knav'ry.
      What, hast thou din'd? The tailor stays thy leisure,

60   To deck thy body with his ruffling treasure.

[Enter Tailor.]

      Come, tailor, let us see these ornaments;
      Lay forth the gown.

[Enter Haberdasher.]

                              What news with you, sir?

Haberdasher

      Here is the cap your worship did bespeak.

Petruchio

      Why, this was moulded on a porringer;

65   A velvet dish. Fie, fie! 'tis lewd and filthy;
      Why, 'tis a cockle or a walnut-shell,
      A knack, a toy, a trick, a baby's cap.
      Away with it. Come, let me have a bigger.

Katherina

      I'll have no bigger; this doth fit the time,

70   And gentlewomen wear such caps as these.

Petruchio
> When you are gentle, you shall have one too,
> And not till then.

Hortensio
> [Aside]   That will not be in haste.

Katherina
> Why, sir, I trust I may have leave to speak;
> And speak I will. I am no child, no babe.
> Your betters have endur'd me say my mind,   75
> And if you cannot, best you stop your ears.
> My tongue will tell the anger of my heart,
> Or else my heart, concealing it, will break;
> And rather than it shall, I will be free
> Even to the uttermost, as I please, in words.   80

Petruchio
> Why, thou say'st true; it is a paltry cap,
> A custard-coffin, a bauble, a silken pie;
> I love thee well in that thou lik'st it not.

Katherina
> Love me or love me not, I like the cap;
> And it I will have, or I will have none.   85

[Exit Haberdasher.]

Petruchio
> Thy gown? Why, ay. Come, tailor, let us see't.
> O mercy, God! what masquing stuff is here?
> What's this? A sleeve? 'Tis like a demi-cannon.
> What, up and down, carv'd like an apple-tart?
> Here's snip and nip and cut and slish and slash,   90
> Like to a censer in a barber's shop.
> Why, what a devil's name, tailor, call'st thou this?

Hortensio
> [Aside] I see she's like to have neither cap nor gown.

Tailor
> You bid me make it orderly and well,
> According to the fashion and the time.   95

Petruchio
> Marry, and did; but if you be rememb'red,

I did not bid you mar it to the time.
Go, hop me over every kennel home,
For you shall hop without my custom, sir.
100   I'll none of it; hence! make your best of it.
Katherina
I never saw a better fashion'd gown,
More quaint, more pleasing, nor more commendable;
Belike you mean to make a puppet of me.
Petruchio
Why, true; he means to make a puppet of thee.
Tailor
105   She says your worship means to make a puppet of her.
Petruchio
O monstrous arrogance! Thou liest, thou thread, thou
    thimble,
Thou yard, three-quarters, half-yard, quarter, nail,
Thou flea, thou nit, thou winter-cricket thou –
Brav'd in mine own house with a skein of thread!
110   Away, thou rag, thou quantity, thou remnant;
Or I shall so bemete thee with thy yard
As thou shalt think on prating whilst thou liv'st!
I tell thee, I, that thou hast marr'd her gown.
Tailor
Your worship is deceiv'd; the gown is made
115   Just as my master had direction.
Grumio gave order how it should be done.
Grumio
I gave him no order; I gave him the stuff.
Tailor
But how did you desire it should be made?
Grumio
Marry, sir, with needle and thread.
Tailor
120   But did you not request to have it cut?
Grumio
Thou hast fac'd many things.

Tailor

I have.

Grumio

Face not me. Thou hast brav'd many men; brave not
me. I will neither be fac'd nor brav'd. I say unto thee, I
bid thy master cut out the gown; but I did not bid him 125
cut it to pieces. Ergo, thou liest.

Tailor

Why, here is the note of the fashion to testify.

Petruchio

Read it.

Grumio

The note lies in's throat, if he say I said so.

Tailor

[*Reads*] 'Imprimis, a loose-bodied gown' – 130

Grumio

Master, if ever I said loose-bodied gown, sew me in
the skirts of it and beat me to death with a bottom of
brown bread; I said a gown.

Petruchio

Proceed.

Tailor

[*Reads*] 'With a small compass'd cape' – 135

Grumio

I confess the cape.

Tailor

[*Reads*] 'With a trunk sleeve' –

Grumio

I confess two sleeves.

Tailor

[*Reads*] 'The sleeves curiously cut.'

Petruchio

Ay, there's the villainy. 140

Grumio

Error i' th' bill, sir; error i' th' bill! I commanded the
sleeves should be cut out, and sew'd up again; and that
I'll prove upon thee, though thy little finger be armed
in a thimble.

Tailor

145 This is true that I say; an I had thee in place where,
     thou shouldst know it.

Grumio

     I am for thee straight; take thou the bill, give me thy
     mete-yard, and spare not me.

Hortensio

     God-a-mercy, Grumio! Then he shall have no odds.

Petruchio

150 Well, sir, in brief, the gown is not for me.

Grumio

     You are i' th' right, sir; 'tis for my mistress.

Petruchio

     Go, take it up unto thy master's use.

Grumio

     Villain, not for thy life! Take up my mistress' gown for
     thy master's use!

Petruchio

155 Why, sir, what's your conceit in that?

Grumio

     O, sir, the conceit is deeper than you think for.
     Take up my mistress' gown to his master's use!
     O fie, fie, fie!

Petruchio

     [Aside] Hortensio, say thou wilt see the tailor paid. –

160 Go take it hence; be gone, and say no more.

Hortensio

     Tailor, I'll pay thee for thy gown to-morrow;
     Take no unkindness of his hasty words.
     Away, I say; commend me to thy master.

[Exit Tailor.]

Petruchio

     Well, come, my Kate; we will unto your father's

165 Even in these honest mean habiliments;
     Our purses shall be proud, our garments poor;
     For 'tis the mind that makes the body rich;

And as the sun breaks through the darkest clouds,
So honour peereth in the meanest habit.
What, is the jay more precious than the lark   170
Because his feathers are more beautiful?
Or is the adder better than the eel
Because his painted skin contents the eye?
O no, good Kate; neither art thou the worse
For this poor furniture and mean array.   175
If thou account'st it shame, lay it on me;
And therefore frolic; we will hence forthwith
To feast and sport us at thy father's house.
Go call my men, and let us straight to him;
And bring our horses unto Long-lane end;   180
There will we mount, and thither walk on foot.
Let's see; I think 'tis now some seven o'clock,
And well we may come there by dinner-time.

Katherina

I dare assure you, sir, 'tis almost two,
And 'twill be supper-time ere you come there.   185

Petruchio

It shall be seven ere I go to horse.
Look what I speak, or do, or think to do,
You are still crossing it. Sirs, let't alone;
I will not go to-day; and ere I do,
It shall be what o'clock I say it is.   190

Hortensio

Why, so this gallant will command the sun.

[*Exeunt.*]

Scene IV

Padua. Before Baptista's house.

[Enter TRANIO *as Lucentio, and the Pedant dress'd like Vincentio.]*

Tranio
    Sir, this is the house; please it you that I call?
Pedant
    Ay, what else? And, but I be deceived,
    Signior Baptista may remember me
    Near twenty years ago in Genoa,
5   Where we were lodgers at the Pegasus.
Tranio
    'Tis well; and hold your own, in any case,
    With such austerity as longeth to a father.

[Enter BIONDELLO.*]*

Pedant
    I warrant you. But, sir, here comes your boy;
    'Twere good he were school'd.
Tranio
10   Fear you not him. Sirrah Biondello,
    Now do your duty throughly, I advise you.
    Imagine 'twere the right Vincentio.
Biondello
    Tut, fear not me.
Tranio
    But hast thou done thy errand to Baptista?
Biondello
15   I told him that your father was at Venice,
    And that you look'd for him this day in Padua.
Tranio
    Th'art a tall fellow; hold thee that to drink.
    Here comes Baptista. Set your countenance, sir.

[Enter BAPTISTA, *and* LUCENTIO *as Cambio.]*

Signior Baptista, you are happily met.
[To the Pedant] Sir, this is the gentleman I told you of;   20
I pray you stand good father to me now;
Give me Bianca for my patrimony.

Pedant

Soft, son!
Sir, by your leave: having come to Padua
To gather in some debts, my son Lucentio   25
Made me acquainted with a weighty cause
Of love between your daughter and himself;
And – for the good report I hear of you,
And for the love he beareth to your daughter,
And she to him – to stay him not too long,   30
I am content, in a good father's care,
To have him match'd; and, if you please to like
No worse than I, upon some agreement
Me shall you find ready and willing
With one consent to have her so bestow'd;   35
For curious I cannot be with you,
Signior Baptista, of whom I hear so well.

Baptista

Sir, pardon me in what I have to say.
Your plainness and your shortness please me well.
Right true it is your son Lucentio here   40
Doth love my daughter, and she loveth him,
Or both dissemble deeply their affections;
And therefore, if you say no more than this,
That like a father you will deal with him,
And pass my daughter a sufficient dower,   45
The match is made, and all is done –
Your son shall have my daughter with consent.

Tranio

I thank you, sir. Where then do you know best
We be affied, and such assurance ta'en
As shall with either part's agreement stand?   50

Baptista

Not in my house, Lucentio, for you know

Pitchers have ears, and I have many servants;
Besides, old Gremio is heark'ning still,
And happily we might be interrupted.
Tranio
55   Then at my lodging, an it like you.
There doth my father lie; and there this night
We'll pass the business privately and well.
Send for your daughter by your servant here;
My boy shall fetch the scrivener presently.
60   The worst is this, that at so slender warning
You are like to have a thin and slender pittance.
Baptista
It likes me well. Cambio, hie you home,
And bid Bianca make her ready straight;
And, if you will, tell what hath happened –
65   Lucentio's father is arriv'd in Padua,
And how she's like to be Lucentio's wife.

[Exit LUCENTIO.*]*

Biondello
I pray the gods she may, with all my heart.
Tranio
Dally not with the gods, but get thee gone.

[Exit BIONDELLO.*]*

Signior Baptista, shall I lead the way?
70   Welcome! One mess is like to be your cheer;
Come, sir; we will better it in Pisa.
Baptista
I follow you.   *[Exeunt.]*

[Re-enter LUCENTIO *as Cambio, and* BIONDELLO.*]*

Biondello
Cambio.
Lucentio
What say'st thou, Biondello?
Biondello
75   You saw my master wink and laugh upon you?

Lucentio

Biondello, what of that?

Biondello

Faith, nothing; but has left me here behind to expound
the meaning or moral of his signs and tokens.

Lucentio

I pray thee moralize them.

Biondello

Then thus: Baptista is safe, talking with the deceiving   80
father of a deceitful son.

Lucentio

And what of him?

Biondello

His daughter is to be brought by you to the supper.

Lucentio

And then?

Biondello

The old priest at Saint Luke's church is at your command   85
at all hours.

Lucentio

And what of all this?

Biondello

I cannot tell, except they are busied about a counterfeit
assurance. Take your assurance of her, cum privilegio
ad imprimendum solum; to th' church take the priest,   90
clerk, and some sufficient honest witnesses.
If this be not that you look for, I have no more to say,
But bid Bianca farewell for ever and a day.

Lucentio

Hear'st thou, Biondello?

Biondello

I cannot tarry. I knew a wench married in an afternoon   95
as she went to the garden for parsley to stuff a rabbit;
and so may you, sir; and so adieu, sir. My master hath
appointed me to go to Saint Luke's to bid the priest be
ready to come against you come with your appendix.

[Exit.]

Lucentio

100   I may and will, if she be so contented.
        She will be pleas'd; then wherefore should I doubt?
        Hap what hap may, I'll roundly go about her;
        It shall go hard if Cambio go without her.

[Exit.]

Scene V

A public road.

[Enter PETRUCHIO, KATHERINA, HORTENSIO, *and*
Servants.]

Petruchio
    Come on, a God's name; once more toward our
        father's.
    Good Lord, how bright and goodly shines the moon!
Katherina
    The moon? The sun! It is not moonlight now.
Petruchio
    I say it is the moon that shines so bright.
Katherina
    I know it is the sun that shines so bright.   5
Petruchio
    Now by my mother's son, and that's myself,
    It shall be moon, or star, or what I list,
    Or ere I journey to your father's house.
    Go on and fetch our horses back again.
    Evermore cross'd and cross'd; nothing but cross'd!   10
Hortensio
    Say as he says, or we shall never go.
Katherina
    Forward, I pray, since we have come so far,
    And be it moon, or sun, or what you please;
    And if you please to call it a rush-candle,
    Henceforth I vow it shall be so for me.   15
Petruchio
    I say it is the moon.
Katherina
                        I know it is the moon.
Petruchio
    Nay, then you lie; it is the blessed sun.
Katherina
    Then, God be bless'd, it is the blessed sun;

But sun it is not, when you say it is not;
20 And the moon changes even as your mind.
What you will have it nam'd, even that it is,
And so it shall be so for Katherine.

Hortensio

Petruchio, go thy ways, the field is won.

Petruchio

Well, forward, forward! thus the bowl should run,
25 And not unluckily against the bias.
But, soft! Company is coming here.

[Enter VINCENTIO.]

[*To* VINCENTIO] Good-morrow, gentle mistress; where
away? –
Tell me, sweet Kate, and tell me truly too,
Hast thou beheld a fresher gentlewoman?
30 Such war of white and red within her cheeks!
What stars do spangle heaven with such beauty
As those two eyes become that heavenly face?
Fair lovely maid, once more good day to thee.
Sweet Kate, embrace her for her beauty's sake.

Hortensio

35 'A will make the man mad, to make a woman of him.

Katherina

Young budding virgin, fair and fresh and sweet,
Whither away, or where is thy abode?
Happy the parents of so fair a child;
Happier the man whom favourable stars
40 Allots thee for his lovely bed-fellow.

Petruchio

Why, how now, Kate, I hope thou art not mad!
This is a man, old, wrinkled, faded, withered,
And not a maiden, as thou sayst he is.

Katherina

Pardon, old father, my mistaking eyes,
45 That have been so bedazzled with the sun
That everything I look on seemeth green;

Now I perceive thou art a reverend father.
Pardon, I pray thee, for my mad mistaking.

Petruchio

Do, good old grandsire, and withal make known
Which way thou travellest – if along with us,   50
We shall be joyful of thy company.

Vincentio

Fair sir, and you my merry mistress,
That with your strange encounter much amaz'd me,
My name is call'd Vincentio, my dwelling Pisa,
And bound I am to Padua, there to visit   55
A son of mine, which long I have not seen.

Petruchio

What is his name?

Vincentio

                    Lucentio, gentle sir.

Petruchio

Happily met; the happier for thy son.
And now by law, as well as reverend age,
I may entitle thee my loving father: 60
The sister to my wife, this gentlewoman,
Thy son by this hath married. Wonder not,
Nor be not grieved – she is of good esteem,
Her dowry wealthy, and of worthy birth;
Beside, so qualified as may beseem   65
The spouse of any noble gentleman.
Let me embrace with old Vincentio;
And wander we to see thy honest son,
Who will of thy arrival be full joyous.

Vincentio

But is this true; or is it else your pleasure,   70
Like pleasant travellers, to break a jest
Upon the company you overtake?

Hortensio

I do assure thee, father, so it is.

Petruchio

Come, go along, and see the truth hereof;
For our first merriment hath made thee jealous.   75

[Exeunt all but HORTENSIO.*]*

Hortensio
Well, Petruchio, this has put me in heart.
Have to my widow; and if she be froward,
Then hast thou taught Hortensio to be untoward.

[Exit.]

ACT FIVE
Scene I

Padua. Before Lucentio's house.

[Enter BIONDELLO, LUCENTIO, and BIANCA; GREMIO is out before.]

Biondello
Softly and swiftly, sir, for the priest is ready.

Lucentio
I fly, Biondello; but they may chance to need thee at
home, therefore leave us.

Biondello
Nay, faith, I'll see the church a your back, and then
come back to my master's as soon as I can.   5

[Exeunt LUCENTIO, BIANCA, and BIONDELLO.]

Gremio
I marvel Cambio comes not all this while.

[Enter PETRUCHIO, KATHERINA, VINCENTIO, GRUMIO, and Attendants.]

Petruchio
Sir, here's the door; this is Lucentio's house;
My father's bears more toward the marketplace;
Thither must I, and here I leave you, sir.

Vincentio
You shall not choose but drink before you go;   10
I think I shall command your welcome here,
And by all likelihood some cheer is toward.

[Knocks.]

Gremio
They're busy within; you were best knock louder.

[Pedant looks out of the window.]

Pedant

What's he that knocks as he would beat down the gate?

Vincentio

15 Is Signior Lucentio within, sir?

Pedant

He's within, sir, but not to be spoken withal.

Vincentio

What if a man bring him a hundred pound or two to make merry withal?

Pedant

Keep your hundred pounds to yourself; he shall need
20 none so long as I live.

Petruchio

Nay, I told you your son was well beloved in Padua. Do you hear, sir? To leave frivolous circumstances, I pray you tell Signior Lucentio that his father is come from Pisa, and is here at the door to speak with him.

Pedant

25 Thou liest: his father is come from Padua, and here looking out at the window.

Vincentio

Art thou his father?

Pedant

Ay, sir; so his mother says, if I may believe her.

Petruchio

[To VINCENTIO] Why, how now, gentleman! Why, this
30 is flat knavery to take upon you another man's name.

Pedant

Lay hands on the villain; I believe 'a means to cozen somebody in this city under my countenance.

[Re-enter BIONDELLO.]

Biondello

I have seen them in the church together. God send 'em good shipping! But who is here? Mine old master,
35 Vincentio! Now we are undone and brought to nothing.

Vincentio

    [Seeing BIONDELLO*]* Come hither, crack-hemp.

Biondello

    I hope I may choose, sir.

Vincentio

    Come hither, you rogue. What, have you forgot me?

Biondello

    Forgot you! No, sir. I could not forget you, for I never
    saw you before in all my life.   40

Vincentio

    What, you notorious villain, didst thou never see thy
    master's father, Vincentio?

Biondello

    What, my old worshipful old master? Yes, marry, sir;
    see where he looks out of the window.

Vincentio

    Is't so, indeed? *[He beats* BIONDELLO*.]*   45

Biondello

    Help, help, help! Here's a madman will murder me.

                                                [Exit.]

Pedant

    Help, son! help, Signior Baptista!

                    [Exit from above.]

Petruchio

    Prithee, Kate, let's stand aside and see the end of this
    controversy.

                    [They stand aside.]

    [Re-enter Pedant below; BAPTISTA, TRANIO, *and*
                    Servants.]

Tranio

    Sir, what are you that offer to beat my servant?   50

Vincentio

    What am I, sir? Nay, what are you, sir? O immortal
    gods! O fine villain! A silken doublet, a velvet hose, a
    scarlet cloak, and a copatain hat! O, I am undone! I am

undone! While I play the good husband at home, my
55 son and my servant spend all at the university.

Tranio

How now! what's the matter?

Baptista

What, is the man lunatic?

Tranio

Sir, you seem a sober ancient gentleman by your habit,
but your words show you a madman. Why, sir, what
60 'cerns it you if I wear pearl and gold? I thank my good
father, I am able to maintain it.

Vincentio

Thy father! O villain! he is a sailmaker in Bergamo.

Baptista

You mistake, sir; you mistake, sir. Pray, what do you
think is his name?

Vincentio

65 His name! As if I knew not his name! I have brought
him up ever since he was three years old, and his name
is Tranio.

Pedant

Away, away, mad ass! His name is Lucentio; and he is
mine only son, and heir to the lands of me, Signior
70 Vincentio.

Vincentio

Lucentio! O, he hath murd'red his master! Lay hold on
him, I charge you, in the Duke's name. O, my son, my
son! Tell me, thou villain, where is my son, Lucentio?

Tranio

Call forth an officer

[Enter One with an Officer.]

75 Carry this mad knave to the gaol. Father Baptista, I
charge you see that he be forthcoming.

Vincentio

Carry me to the gaol!

Gremio
Stay, Officer; he shall not go to prison.
Baptista
Talk not, Signior Gremio; I say he shall go to prison.
Gremio
Take heed, Signior Baptista, lest you be cony-catch'd in   80
this business; I dare swear this is the right Vincentio.
Pedant
Swear if thou dar'st.
Gremio
Nay, I dare not swear it.
Tranio
Then thou wert best say that I am not Lucentio.
Gremio
Yes, I know thee to be Signior Lucentio.   85
Baptista
Away with the dotard; to the gaol with him!
Vincentio
Thus strangers may be hal'd and abus'd. O monstrous
villain!

  [Re-enter BIONDELLO, *with* LUCENTIO *and* BIANCA.]

Biondello
O, we are spoil'd; and yonder he is! Deny him, forswear
him, or else we are all undone.   90

  [Exeunt BIONDELLO, TRANIO, *and Pedant, as fast as
                  may be.]*

Lucentio
[*Kneeling*] Pardon, sweet father.
Vincentio
                          Lives my sweet son?
Bianca
Pardon, dear father.
Baptista
                  How hast thou offended?
Where is Lucentio?

Lucentio

Here's Lucentio,
Right son to the right Vincentio,
95   That have by marriage made thy daughter mine,
While counterfeit supposes blear'd thine eyne.

Gremio

Here's packing, with a witness, to deceive us all!

Vincentio

Where is that damned villain, Tranio,
That fac'd and brav'd me in this matter so?

Baptista

100   Why, tell me, is not this my Cambio?

Bianca

Cambio is chang'd into Lucentio.

Lucentio

Love wrought these miracles. Bianca's love
Made me exchange my state with Tranio,
While he did bear my countenance in the town;
105   And happily I have arrived at the last
Unto the wished haven of my bliss.
What Tranio did, myself enforc'd him to;
Then pardon him, sweet father, for my sake.

Vincentio

I'll slit the villain's nose that would have sent me to
110   the gaol.

Baptista

[To LUCENTIO] But do you hear, sir?
Have you married my daughter without asking my
good will?

Vincentio

Fear not, Baptista; we will content you, go to; but I will
115   in to be revenged for this villainy.   *[Exit.]*

Baptista

And I to sound the depth of this knavery.   *[Exit.]*

Lucentio

Look not pale, Bianca; thy father will not frown.

[Exeunt LUCENTIO and BIANCA.]

Gremio
    My cake is dough, but I'll in among the rest;
    Out of hope of all but my share of the feast.

[Exit.]

Katherina
    Husband, let's follow to see the end of this ado.   120
Petruchio
    First kiss me, Kate, and we will.
Katherina
    What, in the midst of the street?
Petruchio
    What, art thou asham'd of me?
Katherina
    No, sir; God forbid; but asham'd to kiss.
Petruchio
    Why, then, let's home again. Come, sirrah, let's away.   125
Katherina
    Nay, I will give thee a kiss; now pray thee, love, stay.
Petruchio
    Is not this well? Come, my sweet Kate:
    Better once than never, for never too late.

[Exeunt.]

Scene II

Lucentio's house.

[Enter BAPTISTA, VINCENTIO, GREMIO, *the Pedant,*
LUCENTIO, BIANCA, PETRUCHIO, KATHERINA,
HORTENSIO, *and Widow. The Servants with* TRANIO,
BIONDELLO, *and* GRUMIO, *bringing in a banquet.]*

Lucentio
    At last, though long, our jarring notes agree;
    And time it is when raging war is done
    To smile at scapes and perils overblown.
    My fair Bianca, bid my father welcome,
5   While I with self-same kindness welcome thine.
    Brother Petruchio, sister Katherina,
    And thou, Hortensio, with thy loving widow,
    Feast with the best, and welcome to my house.
    My banquet is to close our stomachs up
10 After our great good cheer. Pray you, sit down;
    For now we sit to chat as well as eat.   *[They sit.]*
Petruchio
    Nothing but sit and sit, and eat and eat!
Baptista
    Padua affords this kindness, son Petruchio.
Petruchio
    Padua affords nothing but what is kind.
Hortensio
15 For both our sakes I would that word were true.
Petruchio
    Now, for my life, Hortensio fears his widow.
Widow
    Then never trust me if I be afeard.
Petruchio
    You are very sensible, and yet you miss my sense:
    I mean Hortensio is afeard of you.
Widow
20 He that is giddy thinks the world turns round.

Petruchio
  Roundly replied.
Katherina
                    Mistress, how mean you that?
Widow
  Thus I conceive by him.
Petruchio
  Conceives by me! How likes Hortensio that?
Hortensio
  My widow says thus she conceives her tale.
Petruchio
  Very well mended. Kiss him for that, good widow.   25
Katherina
  'He that is giddy thinks the world turns round.'
  I pray you tell me what you meant by that.
Widow
  Your husband, being troubled with a shrew,
  Measures my husband's sorrow by his woe;
  And now you know my meaning.   30
Katherina
  A very mean meaning.
Widow
                    Right, I mean you.
Katherina
  And I am mean, indeed, respecting you.
Petruchio
  To her, Kate!
Hortensio
  To her, widow!
Petruchio
  A hundred marks, my Kate does put her down.   35
Hortensio
  That's my office.
Petruchio
  Spoke like an officer – ha' to thee, lad.
                          [Drinks to HORTENSIO.*]*

Baptista
How likes Gremio these quick-witted folks?
Gremio
Believe me, sir, they butt together well.
Bianca
40 Head and butt! An hasty-witted body
Would say your head and butt were head and horn.
Vincentio
Ay, mistress bride, hath that awakened you?
Bianca
Ay, but not frighted me; therefore I'll sleep again.
Petruchio
Nay, that you shall not; since you have begun,
45 Have at you for a bitter jest or two.
Bianca
Am I your bird? I mean to shift my bush,
And then pursue me as you draw your bow.
You are welcome all.

[Exeunt BIANCA, KATHERINA, and Widow.]

Petruchio
She hath prevented me. Here, Signior Tranio,
50 This bird you aim'd at, though you hit her not;
Therefore a health to all that shot and miss'd.
Tranio
O, sir, Lucentio slipp'd me like his greyhound,
Which runs himself, and catches for his master.
Petruchio
A good swift simile, but something currish.
Tranio
55 'Tis well, sir, that you hunted for yourself;
'Tis thought your deer does hold you at a bay.
Baptista
O, O, Petruchio! Tranio hits you now.
Lucentio
I thank thee for that gird, good Tranio.

Hortensio
    Confess, confess; hath he not hit you here?
Petruchio
    'A has a little gall'd me, I confess;   60
    And, as the jest did glance away from me,
    'Tis ten to one it maim'd you two outright.
Baptista
    Now, in good sadness, son Petruchio,
    I think thou hast the veriest shrew of all.
Petruchio
    Well, I say no; and therefore, for assurance,   65
    Let's each one send unto his wife,
    And he whose wife is most obedient,
    To come at first when he doth send for her,
    Shall win the wager which we will propose.
Hortensio
    Content. What's the wager?
Lucentio
                              Twenty crowns.   70
Petruchio
    Twenty crowns!
    I'll venture so much of my hawk or hound,
    But twenty times so much upon my wife.
Lucentio
    A hundred then.
Hortensio
                    Content.
Petruchio
                            A match! 'tis done.
Hortensio
    Who shall begin?
Lucentio
                    That will I.   75
    Go, Biondello, bid your mistress come to me.
Biondello
    I go.

                        [Exit.]

Baptista
Son, I'll be your half Bianca comes.
Lucentio
I'll have no halves; I'll bear it all myself.

[Re-enter BIONDELLO.]

How now! what news?
Biondello
80   Sir, my mistress sends you word
That she is busy and she cannot come.
Petruchio
How! She's busy, and she cannot come!
Is that an answer?
Gremio
                Ay, and a kind one too.
Pray God, sir, your wife send you not a worse.
Petruchio
85 I hope better.
Hortensio
Sirrah Biondello, go and entreat my wife
To come to me forthwith.   *[Exit BIONDELLO.]*
Petruchio
            O, ho! entreat her!
Nay, then she must needs come.
Hortensio
              I am afraid, sir,
Do what you can, yours will not be entreated.

[Re-enter BIONDELLO.]

90 Now, where's my wife?
Biondello
She says you have some goodly jest in hand:
She will not come; she bids you come to her.
Petruchio
Worse and worse; she will not come! O vile,
Intolerable, not to be endur'd!
95 Sirrah Grumio, go to your mistress;

Say I command her come to me.

[Exit GRUMIO.]

Hortensio
  I know her answer.
Petruchio
                                    What?
Hortensio
                                              She will not.
Petruchio
  The fouler fortune mine, and there an end.

[Re-enter KATHERINA.]

Baptista
  Now, by my holidame, here comes Katherina!
Katherina
  What is your will, sir, that you send for me?   100
Petruchio
  Where is your sister, and Hortensio's wife?
Katherina
  They sit conferring by the parlour fire.
Petruchio
  Go, fetch them hither; if they deny to come,
  Swinge me them soundly forth unto their husbands.
  Away, I say, and bring them hither straight.   105

[Exit KATHERINA.]

Lucentio
  Here is a wonder, if you talk of a wonder.
Hortensio
  And so it is. I wonder what it bodes.
Petruchio
  Marry, peace it bodes, and love, and quiet life,
  An awful rule, and right supremacy;
  And, to be short, what not that's sweet and happy.   110
Baptista
  Now fair befall thee, good Petruchio!

The wager thou hast won; and I will add
Unto their losses twenty thousand crowns;
Another dowry to another daughter,
115 For she is chang'd, as she had never been.

Petruchio

Nay, I will win my wager better yet,
And show more sign of her obedience,
Her new-built virtue and obedience.

[Re-enter KATHERINA with BIANCA and Widow.]

See where she comes, and brings your froward wives
120 As prisoners to her womanly persuasion.
Katherine, that cap of yours becomes you not:
Off with that bauble, throw it underfoot.

[KATHERINA complies.]

Widow

Lord, let me never have a cause to sigh.
Till I be brought to such a silly pass!

Bianca

125 Fie! what a foolish duty call you this?

Lucentio

I would your duty were as foolish too;
The wisdom of your duty, fair Bianca,
Hath cost me a hundred crowns since supper-time!

Bianca

The more fool you for laying on my duty.

Petruchio

130 Katherine, I charge thee, tell these headstrong women
What duty they do owe their lords and husbands.

Widow

Come, come, you're mocking; we will have no telling.

Petruchio

Come on, I say; and first begin with her.

Widow

She shall not.

Petruchio

I say she shall. And first begin with her.   135

Katherina

Fie, fie! unknit that threatening unkind brow,
And dart not scornful glances from those eyes
To wound thy lord, thy king, thy governor.
It blots thy beauty as frosts do bite the meads,
Confounds thy fame as whirlwinds shake fair buds,   140
And in no sense is meet or amiable.
A woman mov'd is like a fountain troubled –
Muddy, ill-seeming, thick, bereft of beauty;
And while it is so, none so dry or thirsty
Will deign to sip or touch one drop of it.   145
Thy husband is thy lord, thy life, thy keeper,
Thy head, thy sovereign; one that cares for thee,
And for thy maintenance commits his body
To painful labour both by sea and land,
To watch the night in storms, the day in cold,   150
Whilst thou liest warm at home, secure and safe;
And craves no other tribute at thy hands
But love, fair looks, and true obedience –
Too little payment for so great a debt.
Such duty as the subject owes the prince,   155
Even such a woman oweth to her husband;
And when she is froward, peevish, sullen, sour,
And not obedient to his honest will,
What is she but a foul contending rebel
And graceless traitor to her loving lord?   160
I am asham'd that women are so simple
To offer war where they should kneel for peace;
Or seek for rule, supremacy, and sway,
When they are bound to serve, love, and obey.
Why are our bodies soft and weak and smooth,   165
Unapt to toil and trouble in the world,
But that our soft conditions and our hearts
Should well agree with our external parts?
Come, come, you froward and unable worms!

170   My mind hath been as big as one of yours,
     My heart as great, my reason haply more,
     To bandy word for word and frown for frown;
     But now I see our lances are but straws,
     Our strength as weak, our weakness past compare,
175   That seeming to be most which we indeed least are.
     Then vail your stomachs, for it is no boot,
     And place your hands below your husband's foot;
     In token of which duty, if he please,
     My hand is ready, may it do him ease.

Petruchio

180   Why, there's a wench! Come on, and kiss me, Kate.

Lucentio

     Well, go thy ways, old lad, for thou shalt ha't.

Vincentio

     'Tis a good hearing when children are toward.

Lucentio

     But a harsh hearing when women are froward.

Petruchio

     Come, Kate, we'll to bed.
185   We three are married, but you two are sped.
     [To LUCENTIO*]* 'Twas I won the wager, though you hit
       the white;
     And being a winner, God give you good night!

[Exeunt PETRUCHIO *and* KATHERINA*.]*

Hortensio

     Now go thy ways; thou hast tam'd a curst shrow.

Lucentio

     'Tis a wonder, by your leave, she will be tam'd so.

[Exeunt.]

Shakespeare:
Words and Phrases

adapted from the Collins English Dictionary

abate 1 VERB to abate here means to lessen or diminish ❏ *There lives within the very flame of love/A kind of wick or snuff that will abate it* (*Hamlet 4.7*) 2 VERB to abate here means to shorten ❏ *Abate thy hours* (*A Midsummer Night's Dream 3.2*) 3 VERB to abate here means to deprive ❏ *She hath abated me of half my train* (*King Lear 2.4*)

abjure VERB to abjure means to renounce or give up ❏ *this rough magic I here abjure* (*Tempest 5.1*)

abroad ADV abroad means elsewhere or everywhere ❏ *You have heard of the news abroad* (*King Lear 2.1*)

abrogate VERB to abrogate means to put an end to ❏ *so it shall praise you to abrogate scurrility* (*Love's Labours Lost 4.2*)

abuse 1 NOUN abuse in this context means deception or fraud ❏ *What should this mean? Are all the rest come back?/Or is it some abuse, and no such thing?* (*Hamlet 4.7*) 2 NOUN an abuse in this context means insult or offence ❏ *I will be deaf to pleading and excuses/Nor tears nor prayers shall purchase our abuses* (*Romeo and Juliet 3.1*) 3 NOUN an abuse in this context means using something improperly ❏ *we'll digest/Th'abuse*

of distance (*Henry II Chorus*) 4 NOUN an abuse in this context means doing something which is corrupt or dishonest ❏ *Come, bring them away: if these be good people in a commonweal that do nothing but their abuses in common houses, I know no law: bring them away.* (*Measure for Measure 2.1*)

abuser NOUN the abuser here is someone who betrays, a betrayer ❏ *I ... do attach thee/For an abuser of the world* (*Othello 1.2*)

accent NOUN accent here means language ❏ *In states unborn, and accents yet unknown* (*Julius Caesar 3.1*)

accident NOUN an accident in this context is an event or something that happened ❏ *think no more of this night's accidents* (*A Midsummer Night's Dream 4.1*)

accommodate VERB to accommodate in this context means to equip or to give someone the equipment to do something ❏ *The safer sense will ne'er accommodate/His master thus.* (*King Lear 4.6*)

according ADJ according means sympathetic or ready to agree ❏ *within the scope of choice/Lies* my consent and fair according voice (*Romeo and Juliet* 1.2)

account NOUN account often means judgement (by God) or reckoning ❑ *No reckoning made, but sent to my account/With all my imperfections on my head* (*Hamlet* 1.5)

accountant ADJ accountant here means answerable or accountable ❑ *his offence is… /Accountant to the law* (*Measure for Measure* 2.4)

ace NOUN ace here means one or first referring to the lowest score on a dice ❑ *No die, but an ace, for him; for he is but one./Less than an ace, man; for he is dead; he is nothing.* (*A Midsummer Night's Dream* 5.1)

acquit VERB here acquit means to be rid of or free of. It is related to the verb quit ❑ *I am glad I am so acquit of this tinderbox* (*The Merry Wives of Windsor* 1.3)

afeard ADJ afeard means afraid or frightened ❑ *Nothing afeard of what thyself didst make* (*Macbeth* 1.3)

affiance NOUN affiance means confidence or trust ❑ *O how hast thou with jealousy infected/The sweetness of affiance* (*Henry V* 2.2)

affinity NOUN in this context, affinity means important connections, or relationships with important people ❑ *The Moor replies/That he you hurt is of great fame in Cyprus,/And great affinity* (*Othello* 3.1)

agnize VERB to agnize is an old word that means that you recognize or acknowledge something ❑ *I do agnize/A natural and prompt alacrity I find in hardness* (*Othello* 1.3)

ague NOUN an ague is a fever in which the patient has hot and cold

shivers one after the other ❑ *This is some monster of the isle with four legs, who hath got … an ague* (*The Tempest* 2.2)

alarm, alarum NOUN an alarm or alarum is a call to arms or a signal for soldiers to prepare to fight ❑ *Whence cometh this alarum and the noise?* (*Henry VI part I* 1.4)

Albion NOUN Albion is another word for England ❑ *but I will sell my dukedom,/To buy a slobbery and a dirty farm In that nook-shotten isle of Albion* (*Henry V* 3.5)

all of all PHRASE all of all means everything, or the sum of all things ❑ *The very all of all* (*Love's Labours Lost* 5.1)

amend VERB amend in this context means to get better or to heal ❑ *at his touch… They presently amend* (*Macbeth* 4.3)

anchor VERB if you anchor on something you concentrate on it or fix on it ❑ *My invention … Anchors on Isabel* (*Measure for Measure* 2.4)

anon ADV anon was a common word for soon ❑ *You shall see anon how the murderer gets the love of Gonzago's wife* (*Hamlet* 3.2)

antic 1 ADJ antic here means weird or strange ❑ *I'll charm the air to give a sound/While you perform your antic round* (*Macbeth* 4.1) 2 NOUN in this context antic means a clown or a strange, unattractive creature ❑ *If black, why nature, drawing an antic,/Made a foul blot* (*Much Ado About Nothing* 3.1)

apace ADV apace was a common word for quickly ❑ *Come apace* (*As You Like It* 3.3)

apparel NOUN apparel means clothes or clothing ❏ *one suit of apparel* (*Hamlet 3.2*)

appliance NOUN appliance here means cure ❏ *Diseases desperate grown/By desperate appliance are relieved* (*Hamlet 4.3*)

argument NOUN argument here means a topic of conversation or the subject ❏ *Why 'tis the rarest argument of wonder that hath shot out in our latter times* (*All's Well That Ends Well 2.3*)

arrant ADJ arrant means absolute, complete. It strengthens the meaning of a noun ❏ *Fortune, that arrant whore* (*King Lear 2.4*)

arras NOUN an arras is a tapestry, a large cloth with a picture sewn on it using coloured thread ❏ *Behind the arras I'll convey myself/To hear the process* (*Hamlet 3.3*)

art 1 NOUN art in this context means knowledge ❏ *Their malady convinces/The great essay of art* (*Macbeth 4.3*) 2 NOUN art can also mean skill as it does here ❏ *He ... gave you such a masterly report/For art and exercise in your defence* (*Hamlet 4.7*) 3 NOUN art here means magic ❏ *Now I want/Spirits to enforce, art to enchant* (*The Tempest 5 Epilogue*)

assay 1 NOUN an assay was an attempt, a try ❏ *Make assay./Bow, stubborn knees* (*Hamlet 3.3*) 2 NOUN assay can also mean a test or a trial ❏ *he hath made assay of her virtue* (*Measure for Measure 3.1*)

attend (on/upon) VERB attend on means to wait for or to expect ❏ *Tarry I here, I but attend on death* (*Two Gentlemen of Verona 3.1*)

auditor NOUN an auditor was a member of an audience or someone who listens ❏ *I'll be an auditor* (*A Midsummer Night's Dream 3.1*)

aught NOUN aught was a common word which meant anything ❏ *if my love thou holdest at aught* (*Hamlet 4.3*)

aunt 1 NOUN an aunt was another word for an old woman and also means someone who talks a lot or a gossip ❏ *The wisest aunt telling the saddest tale* (*A Midsummer Night's Dream 2.1*) 2 NOUN aunt could also mean a mistress or a prostitute ❏ *the thrush and the jay/Are summer songs for me and my aunts/While we lie tumbling in the hay* (*The Winter's Tale 4.3*)

avaunt EXCLAM avaunt was a common word which meant go away ❏ *Avaunt, you curs!* (*King Lear 3.6*)

aye ADV here aye means always or ever ❏ *Whose state and honour I for aye allow* (*Richard II 5.2*)

baffle VERB baffle meant to be disgraced in public or humiliated ❏ *I am disgraced, impeached, and baffled here* (*Richard II 1.1*)

bald ADJ bald means trivial or silly ❏ *I knew 'twould a bald conclusion* (*The Comedy of Errors 2.2*)

ban NOUN a ban was a curse or an evil spell ❏ *Sometimes with lunatic bans... Enforce their charity* (*King Lear 2.3*)

barren ADJ barren meant empty or hollow ❏ *now I let go your hand, I am barren.* (*Twelfth Night 1.3*)

base ADJ base is an adjective that means unworthy or dishonourable ❏ *civet is of a baser birth than tar* (*As You Like It 3.2*)

base 1 ADJ base can also mean of low social standing or someone who was not part of the ruling class ❏ *Why brand they us with 'base'?* (*King Lear* 1.2) 2 ADJ here base means poor quality ❏ *Base cousin,/ Darest thou break first?* (*Two Noble Kinsmen* 3.3)

bawdy NOUN bawdy means obscene or rude ❏ *Bloody, bawdy villain!* (*Hamlet* 2.2)

bear in hand PHRASE bear in hand means taken advantage of or fooled ❏ *This I made good to you In our last conference, passed in probation with you/How you were borne in hand* (*Macbeth* 3.1)

beard VERB to beard someone was to oppose or confront them ❏ *Com'st thou to beard me in Denmark?* (*Hamlet* 2.2)

beard, in one's PHRASE if you say something in someone's beard you say it to their face ❏ *I will verify as much in his beard* (*Henry V* 3.2)

beaver NOUN a beaver was a visor on a battle helmet ❏ *O yes, my lord, he wore his beaver up* (*Hamlet* 1.2)

become VERB if something becomes you it suits you or is appropriate to you ❏ *Nothing in his life became him like the leaving it* (*Macbeth* 1.4)

bed, brought to PHRASE to be brought to bed means to give birth ❏ *His wife but yesternight was brought to bed* (*Titus Andronicus* 4.2)

bedabbled ADJ if something is bedabbled it is sprinkled ❏ *Bedabbled with the dew, and torn with briers* (*A Midsummer Night's Dream* 3.2)

Bedlam NOUN Bedlam was a word used for Bethlehem Hospital which was a place the insane were sent to ❏ *The country give me proof and precedent/Of Bedlam beggars* (*King Lear* 2.3)

bed-swerver NOUN a bed-swerver was someone who was unfaithful in marriage, an adulterer ❏ *she's/A bed-swerver* (*Winter's Tale* 2.1)

befall 1 VERB to befall is to happen, occur or take place ❏ *In this same interlude it doth befall/That I present a wall* (*A Midsummer Night's Dream* 5.1) 2 VERB to befall can also mean to happen to someone or something ❏ *fair befall thee and thy noble house* (*Richard III* 1.3)

behoof NOUN behoof was an advantage or benefit ❏ *All our surgeons/Convent in their behoof* (*Two Noble Kinsmen* 1.4)

beldam NOUN a beldam was a witch or old woman ❏ *Have I not reason, beldams as you are?* (*Macbeth* 3.5)

belike ADV belike meant probably, perhaps or presumably ❏ *belike he likes it not* (*Hamlet* 3.2)

bent 1 NOUN bent means a preference or a direction ❏ *Let me work,/For I can give his humour true bent,/And I will bring him to the Capitol* (*Julius Caesar* 2.1) 2 ADJ if you are bent on something you are determined to do it ❏ *for now I am bent to know/By the worst means the worst.* (*Macbeth* 3.4)

beshrew VERB beshrew meant to curse or wish evil on someone ❏ *much beshrew my manners and my pride/If Hermia meant to say Lysander lied* (*A Midsummer Night's Dream* 2.2)

betime (s) ADV betime means early ❑ *To business that we love we rise betime* (*Antony and Cleopatra* 4.4)

bevy NOUN bevy meant type or sort, it was also used to mean company ❑ *many more of the same bevy* (*Hamlet* 5.2)

blazon VERB to blazon something meant to display or show it ❑ *that thy skill be more to blazon it* (*Romeo and Juliet* 2.6)

blind ADJ if you are blind when you do something you are reckless or do not care about the consequences ❑ *are you yet to your own souls so blind/ That two you will war with God by murdering me* (*Richard III* 1.4)

bombast NOUN bombast was wool stuffing (used in a cushion for example) and so it came to mean padded out or long-winded. Here it means someone who talks a lot about nothing in particular ❑ *How now my sweet creature of bombast* (*Henry IV part I* 2.4)

bond 1 NOUN a bond is a contract or legal deed ❑ *Well, then, your bond, and let me see* (*Merchant of Venice* 1.3) 2 NOUN bond could also mean duty or commitment ❑ *I love your majesty/According to my bond* (*King Lear* 1.1)

bottom NOUN here bottom means essence, main point or intent ❑ *Now I see/ The bottom of your purpose* (*All's Well That Ends Well* 3.7)

bounteously ADV bounteously means plentifully, abundantly ❑ *I prithee, and I'll pay thee bounteously* (*Twelfth Night* 1.2)

brace 1 NOUN a brace is a couple or two ❑ *Have lost a brace of kinsmen* (*Romeo and Juliet* 5.3) 2 NOUN if you are in a brace position it means you are ready ❑ *For that it stands not in such warlike brace* (*Othello* 1.3)

brand VERB to mark permanently like the markings on cattle ❑ *the wheeled seat/ Of fortunate Caesar ... branded his baseness that ensued* (*Anthony and Cleopatra* 4.14)

brave ADJ brave meant fine, excellent or splendid ❑ *O brave new world/ That has such people in't* (*The Tempest* 5.1)

brine NOUN brine is sea-water ❑ *He shall drink nought brine, for I'll not show him/ Where the quick freshes are* (*The Tempest* 3.2)

brow NOUN brow in this context means appearance ❑ *doth hourly grow/ Out of his brows* (*Hamlet* 3.3)

burden 1 NOUN the burden here is a chorus ❑ *I would sing my song without a burden* (*As You Like It* 3.2) 2 NOUN burden means load or weight (this is the current meaning) ❑ *the scarfs and the bannerets about thee did manifoldly dissuade me from believing thee a vessel of too great a burden* (*All's Well that Ends Well* 2.3)

buttons, in one's PHRASE this is a phrase that means clear, easy to see ❑ *Tis in his buttons he will carry't* (*The Merry Wives of Windsor* 3.2)

cable NOUN cable here means scope or reach ❑ *The law ... Will give her cable* (*Othello* 1.2)

cadent ADJ if something is cadent it is falling or dropping ❑ *With cadent tears fret channels in her cheeks* (*King Lear* 1.4)

canker VERB to canker is to decay, become corrupt ❑ *And, as with age his body uglier grows,/ So his mind cankers* (The Tempest 4.1)

canon, from the PHRASE from the canon is an expression meaning out of order, improper ❑ *Twas from the canon* (Coriolanus 3.1)

cap-a-pie ADV cap-a-pie means from head to foot, completely ❑ *I am courtier cap-a-pie* (The Winter's Tale 4.4)

carbonadoed ADJ if something is carbonadoed it is cut or scored (scratched) with a knife ❑ *it is your carbonadoed* (All's Well That Ends Well 4.5)

carouse VERB to carouse is to drink at length, party ❑ *They cast their caps up and carouse together* (Anthony and Cleopatra 4.12)

carrack NOUN a carrack was a large old ship, a galleon ❑ *Faith, he tonight hath boarded a land-carrack* (Othello 1.2)

cassock NOUN a cassock here means a military cloak, long coat ❑ *half of the which dare not shake the snow from off their cassocks lest they shake themselves to pieces* (All's Well That Ends Well 4.3)

catastrophe NOUN catastrophe here means conclusion or end ❑ *pat he comes, like the catastrophe of the old comedy* (King Lear 1.2)

cautel NOUN a cautel was a trick or deceptive act ❑ *Perhaps he loves you now/And now no soil not cautel doth besmirch* (Hamlet 1.2)

celerity NOUN celerity was a common word for speed, swiftness ❑ *Hence hath offence his quick celerity/ When it is borne in high authority* (Measure for Measure 4.2)

chafe NOUN chafe meant anger or temper ❑ *this Herculean Roman does become/ The carriage of his chafe* (Anthony and Cleopatra 1.3)

chanson NOUN chanson was an old word for a song ❑ *The first row of the pious chanson will show you more* (Hamlet 2.2)

chapman NOUN a chapman was a trader or merchant ❑ *Not uttered by base sale of chapman's tongues* (Love's Labours Lost 2.1)

chaps, chops NOUN chaps (and chops) was a word for jaws ❑ *Which ne'er shook hands nor bade farewell to him/ Till he unseamed him from the nave to th' chops* (Macbeth 1.2)

chattels NOUN chattels were your moveable possessions. The word is used in the traditional marriage ceremony ❑ *She is my goods, my chattels* (The Taming of the Shrew 3.3)

chide VERB if you are chided by someone you are told off or reprimanded ❑ *Now I but chide, but I should use thee worse* (A Midsummer Night's Dream 3.2)

chinks NOUN chinks was a word for cash or money ❑ *he that can lay hold of her/ Shall have the chinks* (Romeo and Juliet 1.5)

choleric ADJ if something was called choleric it meant that they were quick to get angry ❑ *therewithal unruly waywardness that infirm and choleric years bring with them* (King Lear 1.1)

chuff NOUN a chuff was a miser,

someone who clings to his or her money ❑ *ye fat chuffs* (*Henry IV part I 2.2*)

cipher NOUN cipher here means nothing ❑ *Mine were the very cipher of a function* (*Measure for Measure 2.2*)

circummured ADJ circummured means that something is surrounded with a wall ❑ *He hath a garden circummured with brick* (*Measure for Measure 4.1*)

civet NOUN a civet is a type of scent or perfume ❑ *Give me an ounce of civet* (*King Lear 4.6*)

clamorous ADJ clamorous means noisy or boisterous ❑ *Be clamorous and leap all civil bounds* (*Twelfth Night 1.4*)

clangour, clangor NOUN clangour is a word that means ringing (the sound that bells make) ❑ *Like to a dismal clangour heard from far* (*Henry VI part III 2.3*)

cleave VERB if you cleave to something you stick to it or are faithful to it ❑ *Thy thoughts I cleave to* (*The Tempest 4.1*)

clock and clock, 'twixt PHRASE from hour to hour, without stopping or continuously ❑ *To weep 'twixt clock and clock* (*Cymbeline 3.4*)

close ADJ here close means hidden ❑ *Stand close; this is the same Athenian* (*A Midsummer Night's Dream 3.2*)

cloud NOUN a cloud on your face means that you have a troubled, unhappy expression ❑ *He has cloud in's face* (*Anthony and Cleopatra 3.2*)

cloy VERB if you cloy an appetite you satisfy it ❑ *Other women cloy/The appetites they feed* (*Anthony and Cleopatra 2.2*)

cock-a-hoop, set PHRASE if you set cock-a-hoop you become free of everything ❑ *You will set cock-a-hoop* (*Romeo and Juliet 1.5*)

colours NOUN colours is a word used to describe battle-flags or banners. Sometimes we still say that we nail our colours to the mast if we are stating which team or side of an argument we support ❑ *the approbation of those that weep this lamentable divorce under her colours* (*Cymbeline 1.5*)

combustion NOUN combustion was a word meaning disorder or chaos ❑ *prophesying ... Of dire combustion and confused events* (*Macbeth 2.3*)

comely ADJ if you are or something is comely you or it is lovely, beautiful, graceful ❑ *O, what a world is this, when what is comely/Envenoms him that bears it!* (*As You Like It 2.3*)

commend VERB if you commend yourself to someone you send greetings to them ❑ *Commend me to my brother* (*Measure for Measure 1.4*)

compact NOUN a compact is an agreement or a contract ❑ *what compact mean you to have with us?* (*Julius Caesar 3.1*)

compass 1 NOUN here compass means range or scope ❑ *you would sound me from my lowest note to the top of my compass* (*Hamlet 3.2*) 2 VERB to compass here means to achieve, bring about or make happen ❑ *How now shall this be compassed?/ Canst thou bring me to the party?* (*Tempest 3.2*)

comptible ADJ comptible is an old word meaning sensitive ❑ *I am very comptible, even to the least sinister usage.* (*Twelfth Night 1.5*)

confederacy NOUN a confederacy is a group of people usually joined together to commit a crime. It is another word for a conspiracy ❑ *Lo, she is one of this confederacy!* (*A Midsummer Night's Dream 3.2*)

confound VERB if you confound something you confuse it or mix it up; it also means to stop or prevent ❑ *A million fail, confounding oath on oath.* (*A Midsummer Night's Dream 3.2*)

contagion NOUN contagion is an old word for disease or poison ❑ *hell itself breathes out/Contagion to this world* (*Hamlet 3.2*)

contumely NOUN contumely is an old word for an insult ❑ *the proud man's contumely* (*Hamlet 3.1*)

counterfeit 1 VERB if you counterfeit something you copy or imitate it ❑ *Meantime your cheeks do counterfeit our roses* (*Henry VI part I 2.4*) 2 VERB in this context counterfeit means to pretend or make believe ❑ *I will counterfeit the bewitchment of some popular man* (*Coriolanus*)

coz NOUN coz was a shortened form of the word cousin ❑ *sweet my coz, be merry* (*As You Like It 1.2*)

cozenage NOUN cozenage is an old word meaning cheating or a deception ❑ *Thrown out his angle for my proper life,/And with such coz'nage* (*Hamlet 5.2*)

crave VERB crave used to mean to beg or request ❑ *I crave your pardon* (*The Comedy of Errors 1.2*)

crotchet NOUN crotchets are strange ideas or whims ❑ *thou hast some strange crotchets in thy head now* (*The Merry Wives of Windsor 2.1*)

cuckold NOUN a cuckold is a man whose wife has been unfaithful to him ❑ *As there is no true cuckold but calamity* (*Twelfth Night 1.5*)

cuffs, go to PHRASE this phrase meant to fight ❑ *the player went to cuffs in the question* (*Hamlet 2.2*)

cup VERB in this context cup is a verb which means to pour drink or fill glasses with alcohol ❑ *cup us til the world go round* (*Anthony and Cleopatra 2.7*)

cur NOUN cur is an insult meaning dog and is also used to mean coward ❑ *Out, dog! out, cur! Thou drivest me past the bounds/Of maiden's patience* (*A Midsummer Night's Dream 3.2*)

curiously ADV in this context curiously means carefully or skilfully ❑ *The sleeves curiously cut* (*The Taming of the Shrew 4.3*)

curry VERB curry means to flatter or to praise someone more than they are worth ❑ *I would curry with Master Shallow that no man could better command his servants* (*Henry IV part II 5.1*)

custom NOUN custom is a habit or a usual practice ❑ *Hath not old custom made this life more sweet/Than that of painted pomp?* (*As You Like It 2.1*)

cutpurse NOUN a cutpurse is an old word for a thief. Men used to carry their money in small bags (purse) that hung from their belts; thieves would cut the purse from the belt and steal their money ❑ *A cutpurse of the empire and the rule* (*Hamlet 3.4*)

dainty ADJ dainty used to mean splendid, fine ❏ *Why, that's my dainty Ariel!* (Tempest 5.1)

dally VERB if you dally with something you play with it or tease it ❏ *They that dally nicely with words may quickly make them wanton* (Twelfth Night 3.1)

damask COLOUR damask is a light-red or pink colour ❏ *Twas just the difference/Betwixt the constant red and mingled damask* (As You Like It 3.5)

dare 1 VERB dare means to challenge or, confront ❏ *He goes before me, and still dares me on* (A Midsummer Night's Dream 3.3) 2 VERB dare in this context means to present, deliver or inflict ❏ *all that fortune, death, and danger dare* (Hamlet 4.4)

darkly ADV darkly was used in this context to mean secretly or cunningly ❏ *I will go darkly to work with her* (Measure for Measure 5.1)

daw NOUN a daw was a slang term for idiot or fool (after the bird jackdaw which was famous for its stupidity) ❏ *Yea, just so much as you may take upon a knife's point and choke a daw withal* (Much Ado About Nothing 3.1)

debile ADJ debile meant weak or feeble ❏ *And debile minister great power* (All's Well That Ends Well 2.3)

deboshed ADJ deboshed was another way of saying corrupted or debauched ❏ *Men so disordered, deboshed and bold* (King Lear 1.4)

decoct VERB to decoct was to heat up, warm something ❏ *Can sodden water,/A drench for sur-reained jades ... Decoct their cold blood to such valiant heat?* (Henry V 3.5)

deep-revolving ADJ deep-revolving here uses the idea that you turn something over in your mind when you are thinking hard about it and so means deep-thinking, meditating ❏ *The deep-revolving Buckingham/ No more shall be the neighbour to my counsels* (Richard III 4.2)

defect NOUN defect here means shortcoming or something that is not right ❏ *Being unprepared/Our will became the servant to defect* (Macbeth 2.1)

degree 1 NOUN degree here means rank, standing or station ❏ *Should a like language use to all degrees,/ And mannerly distinguishment leave out/Betwixt the prince and beggar* (The Winter's Tale 2.1) 2 NOUN in this context, degree means extent or measure ❏ *her offence/Must be of such unnatural degree* (King Lear 1.1)

deify VERB if you deify something or someone you worship it or them as a God ❏ *all.. deifying the name of Rosalind* (As You Like It 3.2)

delated ADJ delated here means detailed ❏ *the scope/Of these delated articles* (Hamlet 1.2)

delicate ADJ if something was described as delicate it meant it was of fine quality or valuable ❏ *thou wast a spirit too delicate* (The Tempest 1.2)

demise VERB in this context demise means to transmit, give or convey ❏ *what state ... Canst thou demise to any child of mine?* (Richard III 4.4)

deplore VERB to deplore means to express with grief or sorrow ❑ *Never more/ Will I my master's tears to you deplore* (*Twelfth Night 3.1*)

depose VERB if you depose someone you make them take an oath, or swear something to be true ❑ *Depose him in the justice of his cause* (*Richard II 1.3*)

depositary NOUN a depositary is a trustee ❑ *Made you ... my depositary* (*King Lear 2.4*)

derive 1 VERB to derive means to comes from or to descend (it usually applies to people) ❑ *No part of it is mine,/ This shame derives itself from unknown loins.* (*Much Ado About Nothing 4.1*) 2 VERB if you derive something from someone you inherit it ❑ *Treason is not inherited ...Or, if we derive it from our friends/ What's that to me?* (*As You Like It 1.3*)

descry VERB to see or catch sight of ❑ *The news is true, my lord. He is descried* (*Anthony and Cleopatra 3.7*)

desert 1 NOUN desert means worth or merit ❑ *That dost in vile misproson shackle up/ My love and her desert* (*All's Well That Ends Well 2.3*) 2 ADJ desert is used here to mean lonely or isolated ❑ *if that love or gold/ Can in this desert place buy entertainment* (*As You LIke It 2.4*)

design 1 VERB to design means to indicate or point out ❑ *we shall see/ Justice design the victor's chivalry* (*Richard II 1.1*) 2 NOUN a design is a plan, an intention or an undertaking ❑ *hinder not the honour of his design* (*All's Well That Ends Well 3.6*)

designment NOUN a designment was a plan or undertaking ❑ *The desperate tempest hath so bang'd the Turks,/ That their designment halts* (*Othello 2.1*)

despite VERB despite here means to spite or attempt to thwart a plan ❑ *Only to despite them I will endeavour anything* (*Much Ado About Nothing 2.2*)

device NOUN a device is a plan, plot or trick ❑ *Excellent, I smell a device* (*Twelfth Night 2.3*)

disable VERB to disable here means to devalue or make little of ❑ *he disabled my judgement* (*As You Like It 5.4*)

discandy VERB here discandy means to melt away or dissolve ❑ *The hearts ... do discandy , melt their sweets* (*Anthony and Cleopatra 4.12*)

disciple VERB to disciple is to teach or train ❑ *He ...was/ Discipled of the bravest* (*All's Well That Ends Well 1.2*)

discommend VERB if you discommend something you criticize it ❑ *my dialect which you discommend so much* (*King Lear 2.2*)

discourse NOUN discourse means conversation, talk or chat ❑ *which part of it I'll waste/ With such discourse as I not doubt shall make it/ Go quick away* (*The Tempest 5.1*)

discover VERB discover used to mean to reveal or show ❑ *the Prince discovered to Claudio that he loved my niece* (*Much Ado About Nothing 1.2*)

disliken VERB disguise, make unlike ❑ *disliken/ The truth of your own seeming* (*The Winter's Tale 4.4*)

dismantle VERB to dismantle is to remove or take away ❑ *Commit a thing so monstrous to dismantle/*

So many folds of favour (*King Lear 1.1*)

disponge VERB disponge means to pour out or rain down ❏ *The poisonous damp of night disponge upon me* (*Anthony and Cleopatra 4.9*)

distrain VERB to distrain something is to confiscate it ❏ *My father's goods are all distrained and sold* (*Richard II 2.3*)

divers ADJ divers is an old word for various ❏ *I will give out divers schedules of my beauty* (*Twelfth Night 1.5*)

doff VERB to doff is to get rid of or dispose ❏ *make our women fight/To doff their dire distresses* (*Macbeth 4.3*)

dog VERB if you dog someone or something you follow them or it closely ❏ *I will rather leave to see Hector than not to dog him* (*Troilus and Cressida 5.1*)

dotage NOUN dotage here means infatuation ❏ *Her dotage now I do begin to pity* (*A Midsummer NIght's Dream 4.1*)

dotard NOUN a dotard was an old fool ❏ *I speak not like a dotard nor a fool* (*Much Ado About Nothing 5.1*)

dote VERB to dote is to love, cherish, care without seeing any fault ❏ *And won her soul; and she, sweet lady, dotes,/Devoutly dotes, dotes in idolatry* (*A Midsummer Night's Dream 1.1*)

doublet NOUN a doublet was a man's close-fitting jacket with short skirt ❏ *Lord Hamlet, with his doublet all unbraced* (*Hamlet 2.1*)

dowager NOUN a dowager is a widow ❏ *Like to a step-dame or a dowage* (*A Midsummer Night's Dream 1.1*)

dowdy NOUN a dowdy was an ugly woman ❏ *Dido was a dowdy* (*Romeo and Juliet 2.4*)

dower NOUN a dower (or dowery) is the riches or property given by the father of a bride to her husband-to-be ❏ *Thy truth then by they dower* (*King Lear 1.1*)

dram NOUN a dram is a tiny amount ❏ *Why, everything adheres together that no dram of a scruple* (*Twelfth Night 3.4*)

drift NOUN drift is a plan, scheme or intention ❏ *Shall Romeo by my letters know our drift* (*Romeo and Juliet 4.1*)

dropsied ADJ dropsied means pretentious ❏ *Where great additions swell's and virtues none/It is a dropsied honour* (*All's Well That Ends Well 2.3*)

drudge NOUN a drudge was a slave, servant ❏ *If I be his cuckold, he's my drudge* (*All's Well That Ends Well 1.3*)

dwell VERB to dwell sometimes meant to exist, to be ❏ *I'd rather dwell in my necessity* (*Merchant of Venice 1.3*)

earnest ADJ an earnest was a pledge to pay or a payment in advance ❏ *for an earnest of a greater honour/He bade me from him call thee Thane of Cawdor* (*Macbeth 1.3*)

ecstasy NOUN madness ❏ *This is the very ecstasy of love* (*Hamlet 2.1*)

edict NOUN law or declaration ❏ *It stands as an edict in destiny.* (*A Midsummer Night's Dream 1.1*)

egall ADJ egall is an old word meaning equal ❏ *companions/Whose souls do bear an egall yoke of love* (*Merchant of Venice 2.4*)

eisel NOUN eisel meant vinegar ❏ *Woo't drink up eisel?* (*Hamlet 5.1*)

eke, eke out VERB eke meant to add to, to increase. Eke out nowadays means to make something last as long as possible – particularly in the sense of making money last a long time ❏ *Still be kind/And eke out our performance with your mind* (*Henry V Chorus*)

elbow, out at PHRASE out at elbow is an old phrase meaning in poor condition – as when your jacket sleeves are worn at the elbow which shows that it is an old jacket ❏ *He cannot, sir. He's out at elbow* (*Measure for Measure 2.1*)

element NOUN elements were thought to be the things from which all things were made. They were: air, earth, water and fire ❏ *Does not our lives consist of the four elements?* (*Twelfth Night 2.3*)

elf VERB to elf was to tangle ❏ *I'll … elf all my hairs in knots* (*King Lear 2.3*)

embassy NOUN an embassy was a message ❏ *We'll once more hear Orsino's embassy.* (*Twelfth Night 1.5*)

emphasis NOUN emphasis here means a forceful expression or strong statement ❏ *What is he whose grief/Bears such an emphasis* (*Hamlet 5.1*)

empiric NOUN an empiric was an untrained doctor sometimes called a quack ❏ *we must not … prostitute our past-cure malady/To empirics* (*All's Well That Ends Well 2.1*)

emulate ADJ emulate here means envious ❏ *pricked on by a most emulate pride* (*Hamlet 1.1*)

enchant VERB to enchant meant to put a magic spell on ❏ *Damn'd as thou art, thou hast enchanted her,/For I'll refer me to all things of sense* (*Othello 1.2*)

enclog VERB to enclog was to hinder something or to provide an obstacle to it ❏ *Traitors enscarped to enclog the guitless keel* (*Othello 1.2*)

endure VERB to endure was to allow or to permit ❏ *and will endure/Our setting down before't.* (*Macbeth 5.4*)

enfranchise VERB if you enfranchised something you set it free ❏ *Do this or this;/Take in that kingdom and enfranchise that;/Perform't, or else we damn thee.'* (*Anthony and Cleopatra 1.1*)

engage VERB to engage here means to pledge or to promise ❏ *This to be true I do engage my life* (*As You Like It 5.4*)

engaol VERB to lock up or put in prison ❏ *Within my mouth you have engaoled my tongue* (*Richard II 1.3*)

engine NOUN an engine was a plot, device or a machine ❏ *their promises, enticements, oaths, tokens, and all these engines, of lust, are not the things they go under* (*All's Well That Ends Well 3.5*)

englut VERB if you were engulfed you were swallowed up or eaten whole ❏ *For certainly thou art so near the gulf,/Thou needs must be englutted.* (*Henry V 4.3*)

enjoined ADJ enjoined describes people joined together for the same reason ❏ *Of enjoined penitents/*

There's four or five (*All's Well That Ends Well 3.5*)

entertain 1 VERB to entertain here means to welcome or receive ❏ *Approach, rich Ceres, her to entertain.* (*The Tempest 4.1*) 2 VERB to entertain in this context means to cherish, hold in high regard or to respect ❏ *and I quake,/ Lest thou a feverous life shouldst entertain/ And six or seven winters more respect/ Than a perpetual honour.* (*Measure for Measure 3.1*) 3 VERB to entertain means here to give something consideration ❏ *But entertain it,/ And though you think me poor, I am the man/ Will give thee all the world.* (*Anthony and Cleopatra 2.7*) 4 VERB to entertain here means to treat or handle ❏ *your highness is not entertained with that ceremonious affection as you were wont* (*King Lear 1.4*)

envious ADJ envious meant spiteful or vindictive ❏ *he shall appear to the envious a scholar* (*Measure for Measure 3.2*)

ere PREP ere was a common word for before ❏ *ere this I should ha' fatted all the region kites* (*Hamlet 2.2*)

err VERB to err means to go astray, to make a mistake ❏ *And as he errs, doting on Hermia's eyes* (*A Midsummer Night's Dream 1.1*)

erst ADV erst was a common word for once or before ❏ *that erst brought sweetly forth/ The freckled cowslip* (*Henry V 5.2*)

eschew VERB if you eschew something you deliberately avoid doing it ❏ *What cannot be eschewed must be embraced* (*The Merry Wives of Windsor 5.5*)

escote VERB to escote meant to pay for, support ❏ *How are they escoted?* (*Hamlet 2.2*)

estimable ADJ estimable meant appreciative ❏ *I could not with such estimable wonder over-far believe that* (*Twelfth Night 2.1*)

extenuate VERB extenuate means to lessen ❏ *Which by no means we may extenuate* (*A Midsummer Night's Dream 1.1*)

fain ADV fain was a common word meaning gladly or willingly ❏ *I would fain prove so* (*Hamlet 2.2*)

fall NOUN in a voice or music fall meant going higher and lower ❏ *and so die/ That strain again! it had a dying fall* (*Twelfth Night 1.1*)

false ADJ false was a common word for treacherous ❏ *this is counter, you false Danish dogs!* (*Hamlet 4.5*)

fare VERB fare means to get on or manage ❏ *I fare well* (*The Taming of the Shrew Introduction 2*)

feign VERB to feign was to make up, pretend or fake ❏ *It is the more like to be feigned* (*Twelfth Night 1.5*)

fie EXCLAM fie was an exclamation of disgust ❏ *Fie, that you'll say so!* (*Twelfth Night 1.3*)

figure VERB to figure was to symbolize or look like ❏ *Wings and no eyes, figure unheedy haste* (*A Midsummer Night's Dream 1.1*)

filch VERB if you filch something you steal it ❏ *With cunning hast thou filch'd my daughter's heart* (*A Midsummer Night's Dream 1.1*)

flout VERB to flout something meant to scorn it ❏ *Why will you suffer her to flout me thus?* (*A Midsummer Night's Dream 3.2*)

fond ADJ fond was a common word meaning foolish ❑ *Shall we their fond pageant see?* (*A Midsummer Night's Dream 3.2*)

footing 1 NOUN footing meant landing on shore, arrival, disembarkation ❑ *Whose footing here anticipates our thoughts/A se'nnight's speed.* (*Othello 2.1*) 2 NOUN footing also means support ❑ *there your charity would have lacked footing* (*Winter's Tale 3.3*)

forsooth ADV in truth, certainly, truly
❑ *I had rather, forsooth, go before you like a man* (*The Merry Wives of Windsor 3.2*)

forswear VERB if you forswear you lie, swear falsely or break your word ❑ *he swore a thing to me on Monday night, which he forswore on Tuesday morning* (*Much Ado About Nothing 5.1*)

freshes NOUN a fresh is a fresh water stream ❑ *He shall drink nought brine, for I'll not show him/Where the quick freshes are.* (*Tempest 3.2*)

furlong NOUN a furlong is a measure of distance. It is the equivalent on one eight of a mile ❑ *Now would I give a thousand furlongs of sea for an acre of barren ground* (*Tempest 1.1*)

gaberdine NOUN a gaberdine is a cloak ❑ *My best way is to creep under his gaberdine* (*Tempest 2.2*)

gage NOUN a gage was a challenge to duel or fight ❑ *There is my gage, Aumerle, in gage to thine* (*Richard II 4.1*)

gait NOUN your gait is your way of walking or step ❑ *I know her by her gait* (*Tempest 4.1*)

gall VERB to gall is to annoy or irritate
❑ *Let it not gall your patience, good Iago,/That I extend my manners* (*Othello 2.1*)

gambol NOUN frolic or play ❑ *Hop in his walks, and gambol in his eyes* (*A Midsummer Night's Dream 3.1*)

gaskins NOUN gaskins is an old word for trousers ❑ *or, if both break, your gaskins fall.* (*Twelfth Night 1.5*)

gentle ADJ gentle means noble or well-born ❑ *thrice-gentle Cassio!* (*Othello 3.4*)

glass NOUN a glass was another word for a mirror ❑ *no woman's face remember/Save from my glass, mine own* (*Tempest 3.1*)

gleek VERB to gleek means to make a joke or jibe ❑ *Nay, I can gleek upon occasion* (*A Midsummer Night's Dream 3.1*)

gust NOUN gust meant taste, desire or enjoyment. We still say that if you do something with gusto you do it with enjoyment or enthusiasm ❑ *the gust he hath in quarrelling* (*Twelfth Night 1.3*)

habit NOUN habit means clothes ❑ *You know me by my habit* (*Henry V 3.6*)

heaviness NOUN heaviness means sadness or grief ❑ *So sorrow's heaviness doth heavier grow/For debt that bankrupt sleep doth sorrow owe* (*A Midsummer Night's Dream 3.2*)

heavy ADJ if you are heavy you are said to be sad or sorrowful ❑ *Away from light steals home my heavy son* (*Romeo and Juliet 1.1*)

hie VERB to hie meant to hurry ❑ *My husband hies him home* (*All Well That Ends Well 4.4*)

hollowly ADV if you did something hollowly you did it insincerely ❏ *If hollowly invert/ What best is boded me to mischief! (Tempest 3.1)*

holy-water, court PHRASE if you court holy water you make empty promises, or make statements which sound good but have no real meaning ❏ *court holy-water in a dry house is better than this rain-water out o'door (King Lear 3.2)*

howsoever ADV howsoever was often used instead of however ❏ *But howsoever strange and admirable (A Midsummer Night's Dream 5.1)*

humour NOUN your humour was your mood, frame of mind or temperament ❏ *it fits my humour well (As You Like It 3.2)*

ill ADJ ill means bad ❏ *I must thank him only,/ Let my remembrance suffer ill report (Antony and Cleopatra 2.2)*

indistinct ADJ inseparable or unable to see a difference ❏ *Even till we make the main and the aerial blue/ An indistinct regard. (Othello 2.1)*

indulgence NOUN indulgence meant approval ❏ *As you from crimes would pardoned be,/ Let your indulgence set me free (The Tempest Epilogue)*

infirmity NOUN infirmity was weakness or fraility ❏ *Be not disturbed with my infirmity (The Tempest 4.1)*

intelligence NOUN here intelligence means information ❏ *Pursue her; and for this intelligence/ If I have thanks (A Midsummer Night's Dream 1.1)*

inwards NOUN inwards meant someone's internal organs ❏ *the thought whereof/ Doth like a poisonous mineral gnaw my inwards (Othello 2.1)*

issue 1 NOUN the issue of a marriage are the children ❏ *To thine and Albany's issues,/ Be this perpetual (King Lear 1.1)* 2 NOUN in this context issue means outcome or result ❏ *I am to pray you, not to strain my speech,/ To grosser issues (Othello)*

kind NOUN kind here means situation or case ❏ *But in this kind, wanting your father's voice,/ The other must be held the worthier. (A Midsummer Night's Dream 1.1)*

knave NOUN a knave was a common word for scoundrel ❏ *How absolute the knave is! (Hamlet 5.1)*

league NOUN A distance. A league was the distance a person could walk in one hour ❏ *From Athens is her house remote seven leagues (A Midsummer Night's Dream 1.1)*

lief, had as ADJ I had as lief means I should like just as much ❏ *I had as lief the town crier spoke my lines (Hamlet 1.2)*

livery NOUN livery was a costume, outfit, uniform usually worn by a servant ❏ *You can endure the livery of a nun (A Midsummer Night's Dream 1.1)*

loam NOUN loam is soil containing decayed vegetable matter and therefore good for growing crops and plants ❏ *and let him have some plaster, or some loam, or some rough-cast about him, to signify wall (A Midsummer Night's Dream 3.1)*

lusty ADJ lusty meant strong ❏ *and oared/ Himself with his good arms in lusty stroke/ To th' shore (The Tempest 2.1)*

maidenhead NOUN maidenhead means chastity or virginity ❑ *What I am, and what I would, are as secret as maidenhead* (*Twelfth Night 1.5*)

mark VERB mark means to note or pay attention to ❑ *Where sighs and groans,/ Are made not marked* (*Macbeth 4.3*)

marvellous ADJ very or extremely ❑ *here's a marvellous convenient place for our rehearsal* (*A Midsummer Night's Dream 3.1*)

meet ADJ right or proper ❑ *tis most meet you should* (*Macbeth 5.1*)

merely ADV completely or entirely ❑ *Love is merely a madness* (*As You Like It 3.2*)

misgraffed ADJ misgraffed is an old word for mismatched or unequal ❑ *Or else misgraffed in respect of years* (*A Midsummer Night's Dream 1.1*)

misprision NOUN a misprision meant an error or mistake ❑ *Misprision in the highest degree!* (*Twelfth Night 1.5*)

mollification NOUN mollification is appeasement or a way of preventing someone getting angry ❑ *I am to hull here a little longer. Some mollification for your giant* (*Twelfth Night 1.5*)

mouth, cold in the PHRASE a well-known saying of the time which meant to be dead ❑ *What, must our mouths be cold?* (*The Tempest 1.1*)

murmur NOUN murmur was another word for rumour or hearsay ❑ *and then 'twas fresh in murmur* (*Twelfth Night 1.2*)

murrain NOUN murrain was another word for plague, pestilence ❑ *A murrain on your monster, and the devil take your fingers!* (*The Tempest 3.2*)

neaf NOUN neaf meant fist ❑ *Give me your neaf, Monsieur Mustardseed* (*A Midsummer Night's Dream 4.1*)

nice 1 ADJ nice had a number of meanings here it means fussy or particular ❑ *An therefore, goaded with most sharp occasions,/ Which lay nice manners by, I put you to/ The use of your own virtues* (*All's Well That Ends Well 5.1*) 2 ADJ nice here means critical or delicate ❑ *We're good... To set so rich a man/ On the nice hazard of one doubtful hour?* (*Henry IV part 1*) 3 ADJ nice in this context means carefully accurate, fastidious ❑ *O relation/ Too nice and yet too true!* (*Macbeth 4.3*) 4 ADJ trivial, unimportant ❑ *Romeo .. Bid him bethink/ How nice the quarrel was* (*Romeo and Juliet 3.1*)

nonpareil NOUN if you are nonpareil you are without equal, peerless ❑ *though you were crown'd/ The nonpareil of beauty!* (*Twelfth Night 1.5*)

office NOUN office here means business or work ❑ *Speak your office* (*Twelfth Night 1.5*)

outsport VERB outsport meant to overdo ❑ *Let's teach ourselves that honorable stop,/ Not to outsport discretion.* (*Othello 2.2*)

owe VERB owe meant own, possess ❑ *Lend less than thou owest* (*King Lear 1.4*)

paragon 1 VERB to paragon was to surpass or excede ❑ *he hath achieved a maid/ That paragons description and wild fame* (*Othello 2.1*) 2 VERB to paragon could also mean to compare with ❑ *I will give thee* *bloody teeth If thou with Caesar paragon again/My man of men* (*Anthony and Cleopatra* 1.5)

pate NOUN pate is another word for head ❏ *Back, slave, or I will break thy pate across* (*The Comedy of Errors* 2.1)

paunch VERB to paunch someone is to stab (usually in the stomach). Paunch is still a common word for a stomach ❏ *Batter his skull, or paunch him with a stake* (*The Tempest* 3.2)

peevish ADJ if you are peevish you are irritable or easily angered ❏ *Run after that same peevish messenger* (*Twelfth Night* 1.5)

peradventure ADV perhaps or maybe ❏ *Peradventure this is not Fortune's work* (*As You Like It* 1.2)

perforce 1 ADV by force or violently ❏ *my rights and royalties,/Plucked from my arms perforce* (*Richard II* 2.3) 2 ADV necessarily ❏ *The hearts of men, they must perforce have melted* (*Richard II* 5.2)

personage NOUN personage meant your appearance ❏ *Of what personage and years is he?* (*Twelfth Night* 1.5)

pestilence NOUN pestilence was a common word for plague or disease ❏ *Methought she purg'd the air of pestilence!* (*Twelfth Night* 1.1)

physic NOUN physic was medicine or a treatment ❏ *tis a physic/That's bitter to sweet end* (*Measure for Measure* 4.6)

place NOUN place means a person's position or rank ❏ *Sons, kinsmen, thanes,/And you whose places are the nearest* (*Macbeth* 1.4)

post NOUN here a post means a messenger ❏ *there are twenty weak and wearied posts/Come from the north* (*Henry IV part II* 2.4)

pox NOUN pox was a word for any disease during which the victim had blisters on the skin. It was also a curse, a swear word ❏ *The pox of such antic, lisping, affecting phantasims* (*Romeo and Juliet* 2.4)

prate VERB to prate means to chatter ❏ *if thou prate of mountains* (*Hamlet* 5.1)

prattle VERB to prattle is to chatter or talk without purpose ❏ *I prattle out of fashion, and I dote In mine own comforts* (*Othello* 2.1)

precept NOUN a precept was an order or command ❏ *and my father's precepts I therein do forget.* (*The Tempest* 3.1)

present ADJ present here means immediate ❏ *We'll put the matter to the present push* (*Hamlet* 5.1)

prithee EXCLAM prithee is the equivalent of please or may I ask – a polite request ❏ *I prithee, and I'll pay thee bounteously* (*Twelfth Night* 1.2)

prodigal NOUN a prodigal is someone who wastes or squanders money ❏ *he's a very fool, and a prodigal* (*Twelfth Night* 1.3)

purpose NOUN purpose is used here to mean intention ❏ *understand my purposes aright* (*King Lear* 1.4)

quaff VERB quaff was a common word which meant to drink heavily or take a big drink ❏ *That quaffing and drinking will undo you* (*Twelfth Night* 1.3)

quaint 1 ADJ clever, ingenious ❑ *with a quaint device* (*The Tempest 3.3*) 2 ADJ cunning ❑ *I'll… tell quaint lies* (*Merchant of Venice 3.4*) 3 ADJ pretty, attractive ❑ *The clamorous owl, that nightly hoots and wonders/At our quaint spirit* (*A Midsummer Night's Dream 2.2*)

quoth VERB an old word which means say ❑ *'Tis dinner time.' quoth I* (*The Comedy of Errors 2.1*)

rack NOUN a rack described clouds or a cloud formation ❑ *And, like this insubstantial pageant faded,/ Leave not a rack behind* (*The Tempest 4.1*)

rail VERB to rant or swear at. It is still used occasionally today ❑ *Why do I rail on thee* (*Richard II 5.5*)

rate NOUN rate meant estimate, opinion ❑ *My son is lost, and, in my rate, she too* (*The Tempest 2.1*)

recreant NOUN recreant is an old word which means coward ❑ *Come, recreant, come, thou child* (*A Midsummer Night's Dream 3.2*)

remembrance NOUN remembrance is used here to mean memory or recollection ❑ *our remembrances of days foregone* (*All's Well That Ends Well 1.3*)

resolute ADJ firm or not going to change your mind ❑ *You are resolute, then?* (*Twelfth Night 1.5*)

revels NOUN revels means celebrations or a party ❑ *Our revels now are ended* (*The Tempest 4.1*)

rough-cast NOUN a mixture of lime and gravel (sometimes shells too) for use on an outer wall ❑ *and let him have some plaster, or some loam, or some rough-cast about him, to signify wall* (*A Midsummer Night's Dream 3.1*)

sack NOUN sack was another word for wine ❑ *My man-monster hath drowned his tongue in sack.* (*The Tempest 3.2*)

sad ADJ in this context sad means serious, grave ❑ *comes me the Prince and Claudio… in sad conference* (*Much Ado About Nothing 1.3*)

sampler NOUN a piece of embroidery, which often showed the family tree ❑ *Both on one sampler, sitting on one cushion* (*A Midsummer Night's Dream 3.2*)

saucy ADJ saucy means rude ❑ *I heard you were saucy at my gates* (*Twelfth Night 1.5*)

schooling NOUN schooling means advice ❑ *I have some private schooling for you both.* (*A Midsummer Night's Dream 1.1*)

seething ADJ seething in this case means boiling – we now use seething when we are very angry ❑ *Lovers and madmen have such seething brains* (*A Midsummer Night's Dream 5.1*)

semblative ADJ semblative means resembling or looking like ❑ *And all is semblative a woman's part.* (*Twelfth Night 1.4*)

several ADJ several here means separate or different ❑ *twenty several messengers* (*Anthony and Cleopatra 1.5*)

shrew NOUN An annoying person or someone who makes you cross ❑ *Bless you, fair shrew.* (*Twelfth Night 1.3*)

shroud VERB to shroud is to hide or shelter ❏ *I will here, shroud till the dregs of the storm be past* (*The Tempest 2.2*)

sickleman NOUN a sickleman was someone who used a sickle to harvest crops ❏ *You sunburnt sicklemen, of August weary* (*The Tempest 4.1*)

soft ADV soft here means wait a moment or stop ❏ *But, soft, what nymphs are these* (*A Midsummer Night's Dream 4.1*)

something ADV something here means somewhat or rather ❏ *Be something scanter of your maiden presence* (*Hamlet 1.3*)

sooth NOUN truly ❏ *Yes, sooth; and so do you* (*A Midsummer Night's Dream 3.2*)

spleen NOUN spleen means fury or anger ❏ *That, in a spleen, unfolds both heaven and earth* (*A Midsummer Night's Dream 1.1*)

sport NOUN sport means recreation or entertainment ❏ *I see our wars/ Will turn unto a peaceful comic sport* (*Henry VI part I 2.2*)

strain NOUN a strain is a tune or a musical phrase ❏ *and so die/That strain again! it had a dying fall* (*Twelfth Night 1.1*)

suffer VERB in this context suffer means perish or die ❏ *but an islander that hath lately suffered by a thunderbolt.* (*The Tempest 2.2*)

suit NOUN a suit is a petition, request ˙or proposal (marriage) ❏ *Because she will admit no kind of suit* (*Twelfth Night 1.2*)

sup VERB to sup is to have supper ❏ *Go know of Cassio where he supped tonight* (*Othello 5.1*)

surfeit NOUN a surfeit is an amount which is too large ❏ *If music be the food of love, play on;/Give me excess of it, that, surfeiting,/The appetite may sicken* (*Twelfth Night 1.1*)

swain NOUN a swain is a suitor or person who wants to marry ❏ *take this transformed scalp/From off the head of this Athenian swain* (*A Midsummer Night's Dream 4.1*)

thereto ADV thereto meant also ❏ *If she be black, and thereto have a wit* (*Othello 2.1*)

throstle NOUN a throstle was a name for a song-bird ❏ *The throstle with his note so true* (*A Midsummer Night's Dream 3.1*)

tidings NOUN tidings meant news ❏ *that upon certain tidings now arrived, importing the mere perdition of the Turkish fleet* (*Othello 2.2*)

transgress VERB if you transgress you break a moral law or rule of behaviour ❏ *Virtue that transgresses is but patched with sin* (*Twelfth Night 1.5*)

troth, by my PHRASE this phrase means I swear or in truth or on my word ❏ *By my troth, Sir Toby, you must come in earlier o' nights* (*Twelfth Night 1.3*)

trumpery NOUN trumpery means things that look expensive but are worth nothing (often clothing) ❏ *The trumpery in my house, go bring it hither/For stale catch these thieves* (*The Tempest 4.1*)

twink NOUN In the wink of an eye or no time at all ❏ *Ay, with a twink* (*The Tempest 4.1*)

undone ADJ if something or someone is undone they are ruined, destroyed, brought down ❑ *You have undone a man of fourscore three* (*The Winter's Tale 4.4*)

varlets NOUN varlets were villains or ruffians ❑ *Say again: where didst thou leave these varlets?* (*The Tempest 4.1*)

vaward NOUN the vaward is an old word for the vanguard, front part or earliest ❑ *And since we have the vaward of the day* (*A Midsummer Night's Dream 4.1*)

visage NOUN face ❑ *when Phoebe doth behold/ Her silver visage in the watery glass* (*A Midsummer Night's Dream 1.1*)

voice NOUN voice means vote ❑ *He has our voices* (*Coriolanus 2.3*)

waggish ADJ waggish means playful ❑ *As waggish boys in game themselves forswear* (*A Midsummer Night's Dream 1.1*)

wane VERB to wane is to vanish, go down or get slighter. It is most often used to describe a phase of the moon ❑ *but, O, methinks, how slow/ This old moon wanes* (*A Midsummer Night's Dream 1.1*)

want VERB to want means to lack or to be without ❑ *a beast that wants discourse of reason/ Would have mourned longer* (*Hamlet 1.2*)

warrant VERB to assure, promise, guarantee ❑ *I warrant your grace* (*As You Like It 1.2*)

welkin NOUN welkin is an old word for the sky or the heavens ❑ *The starry welkin cover thou anon/ With drooping fog as black as Acheron* (*A Midsummer Night's Dream 3.2*)

wench NOUN wench is an old word for a girl ❑ *Well demanded, wench* (*The Tempest 1.2*)

whence ADV from where ❑ *Whence came you, sir?* (*Twelfth Night 1.5*)

wherefore ADV why ❑ *Wherefore, sweetheart? what's your metaphor?* (*Twelfth Night 1.3*)

wide-chopped ADJ if you were wide-chopped you were big-mouthed ❑ *This wide-chopped rascal* (*The Tempest 1.1*)

wight NOUN wight is an old word for person or human being ❑ *She was a wight, if ever such wight were* (*Othello 2.1*)

wit NOUN wit means intelligence or wisdom ❑ *thou didst conclude hairy men plain dealers, without wit* (*The Comedy of Errors 2.2*)

wits NOUN wits mean mental sharpness ❑ *we that have good wits have much to answer for* (*As You Like It 4.1*)

wont ADJ to wont is to be in the habit of doing something regularly ❑ *When were you wont to use my sister thus?* (*The Comedy of Errors 2.2*)

wooer NOUN a wooer is a suitor, someone who is hoping to marry ❑ *and of a foolish knight that you brought in one night here to be her wooer* (*Twelfth Night 1.3*)

wot VERB wot is an old word which means know or learn ❑ *for well I wot/ Thou runnest before me* (*A Midsummer Night's Dream 3.2*)